THE MONEY PLAN

THE
MONEY PLAN

CREATING WEALTH INDEPENDENCE
FOR A SECURE FUTURE

Steven J. Lee

NEW YORK

Vantage Point Books and the Vantage Point Books colophon are
registered trademarks of Vantage Press, Inc.

FIRST EDITION: June 2011

Published by Vantage Point Books

Vantage Press, Inc.

419 Park Avenue South

New York, NY 10016

www.vantagepointbooks.com

Manufactured in the United States of America

ISBN: 978-1-936467-00-6

Library of Congress Cataloging-in-Publication data are on file.

0 9 8 7 6 5 4 3 2 1

Cover and Interior design by Pauline Neuwirth

This book is dedicated to my wife, Karen Athena Lee, who has been through the lean time that brought us prosperity and given us two wonderful children in Justin and Megan.

Blue Eyes

Blue Eyes has butterflies
on spring flower blooms,
In the pursing of her lips
she hums a song of bees,
Not bothered by the wind
she gathers rustling leaves,
Those Blue Eyes gleam so
they push away the night,
Like some star-like silver
Minerva's eyes on fire.

CONTENTS

ACKNOWLEDGMENTS

I am grateful to many individuals who have helped in the research and endless rewrites of this book. Their input has guided me in selecting appropriate material and eliminating unsuitable content.

Special thanks go my lay readers, Linda Tweedie, Nat Krate, Paul Joubert, Larry Knowlton, Dennis Doughty, Jaime Katz, Megan Lee, Barbara Blanchard, William Stangel, Bruce Katz, Mel Schreiber, Justin Lee, Alan Nash and of course Karen Lee. With their help it has been possible to test the readability of the presentations so that most everyone can understand the underlying message.

In addition, my patient editors Hal Clifford and Larissa Hordynsky spent many hours keeping themes intact and on track. Also, one could not ask for a better publisher than David Lamb or editorial director than Joe Pittman. Pauline Neuwirth and her staff did a great job of graphic design with very difficult material.

It would be unkind of me not to acknowledge the thousands of Internet sites I visited during the last two years, and their abundance of excellent financial materials. The genius of those who designed the Internet is proof that planning and execution are the keys to achievement.

INTRODUCTION

It has been nearly four decades since I first entered the workaday world and decided to accumulate the means to ride out any financial storm, retire earlier than most people, and leave enough of an estate to assure some security to my future family. In that time, two things have been demonstrated to me beyond a doubt. First, the pathway for achieving high compensation entails education and leadership skills. Second, very few people seem to be investing income wisely, even though it is the companion ingredient for building affluence.

Some people argue that success is just a matter of luck—of being in the right place at the right time. That argument should be rejected. The truth is that worthwhile accomplishments require reasoned analysis, minimization of risk, and constant preparation. Prudent planning produces intended outcomes, whereas passive efforts most often produce missed opportunity and failure.

I have attended numerous lectures on rapid wealth building with no money down real estate or buying surplus government equipment at a fraction of its resale value. My conclusion is that these seminars prove that light travels faster than sound. This is why these programs appear bright until you hear the promoter speak about their concept.

There are many fanciful books on investing with promises to get rich quickly. I have read some of them with amusement, and my take is that there are no tricks or shortcuts that work for the majority of people. Chances of hitting the jackpot are zero. I have seen some far out claims like:

Make Millions in Real Estate With No Money Down
Marketing Millions In Days
Millionaire in 100 Days: The Daily Plan
Get Rich Now Without Effort
One of the World's Greatest Investors Shares All His Easy Secrets

Over the years I have become a very worn-out get-rich-quicker. That means I recognize that if someone is advertising that they can give me a hidden secret about making lots of money, for some of my money, they really only want to get my money.

At the other end of the spectrum are the well-meaning writers who throw the entire pot of financial alphabet soup at their pages. It falls to the reader to clean up the mess and decide what to digest. These can be good reference works, but the Internet contains most of this knowledge so they tend to have very limited utility.

In the preface to a book about financial management for women that I wrote in 1979, I observed that since "many women have a problem with money management," they often fail at "capital accumulation." Since that time I have learned that both men and women have the same shortage of knowledge on how to invest their money safely and wisely. One of the most important knowledge bases is how to handle money, and it's the area where the large majority of adults are weakest. Money is a round commodity all too prone to rolling away. *The Money Plan* will get you started along the road to wealth if you apply yourself. These pages present a systematic **Plan** for acquiring wealth, managing assets, and investing astutely.

I suggest that before making any computations on the worksheets included in *The Money Plan* you read the entire text and get comfortable with its contents. As you study alternative investments and examine your present situation, you will develop ideas about how to go about investing your hard-earned money. Once that overview is completed, you will make the most effective use of the worksheets, guidelines, and the suggested record-keeping systems.

We are in a new financial environment, but the rules discussed in *The Money Plan* are as essential today as they were many decades ago. Proper money management is about learning the language of markets, the structure that is right for you, setting goals and planning to accomplish them. *The Money Plan* is a convenient jumping-off point for what has worked for me and quite possibly will work just as well for you.

It is my hope that *The Money Plan* goes the extra mile in laying out something in the way of a **Plan** that can be followed and used by most people who want to learn, have a computer, and earn a decent living. I hope you come to think of this book as sort of a successful uncle who is trying to show you the ropes about using money to create family wealth.

THE MONEY PLAN

1

FINANCIAL COMMANDMENTS

Our high schools and universities instruct in most aspects of how to be a professional engineer, doctor, lawyer, computer designer, software designer, and business executive, as well as a wide range of other skill sets required in a complex society. Left out of the mix is the preparation for basic finance and capital management. Many people cannot balance their checking account, don't budget, make impulse purchases, don't read financial publications, fail to study their brokerage or 401(k) statements and wonder why they are always broke ... or perhaps running in place.

Those who pursue rigorous training are often doing so out of a desire to increase their earning capacity and produce a better life for themselves and their family. In these pages a coherent **PLAN** for savings and long-term wealth generation is presented in a step-by-step fashion. It's not the only way to achieve this goal but it is a tried-and-true methodology that has survived some thirty years of testing. Most media outlets push higher wage earners to squander their savings instinct in favor of consumption of the latest fad in goods and services. The practical aspect of need fulfillment becomes lost in a temporary diversion with little gain in comfort or improved lifestyle.

The fundamental guidelines of producing wealth by successful resource management are difficult to locate, learn, and apply in books that present every possible alternative without drawing a conclusion on what to select. The Internet contains most everything, but then one needs to know where to navigate and how to piece it all together. If you are willing to apply yourself with determination and stick to our **PLAN**, you can learn what you need to know and make it work for you.

THE FIFTEEN COMMANDMENTS OF MONEY

There probably should have been a second set of commandments for Moses to carry down the mountain along with the original Ten Commandments. These might be called the money commandments, whose dissemination seems to have been largely forgotten somewhere along the pathway of history. That does not make them insignificant to your pecuniary life. Cash in the bank, a strong net worth, retirement on your own terms, children well educated, and sensible investing have sound principles behind them. The money commandments might read something like this:

FIFTEEN MONEY COMMANDMENTS

I. The first rule in making money is not to lose it.
II. Thou shalt not forget that money is only money and not character or fame.
III. Thou shalt honor experienced people who have money, and profit from their knowledge.

IV. Thou shalt not worship thy investment advisor, for if she were so smart she would be retired by now.

V. Many rogues swear falsely about secret opportunities, but only generating real profit is the chosen path to making money.

VI. Thy parents and relatives shall not be thy bankers.

VII. Thou shalt not covet what thou art not willing to work for.

VIII. Thou shalt not swear at thy fate when things go badly but roll up thy sleeves and get back to work. (No one's listening anyway.)

IX. Thou shalt not carry a credit card balance as this puts you in the devil's grasp.

X. Thou shalt not compromise principles just to reap a sum of money.

XI. Thou shalt avoid the false idols of the news and money press and follow thine own mind.

XII. Thou shalt not be afraid to risk thy money but be mindful of possible consequences if a loss ensues.

XIII. Money saved in store sales at the holidays is money thou hast earned.

XIV. At life's end thy money shall not accompany thee onward.

XV. The closer thy life is to owning things outright without debt, the closer thou art to heavenly bliss.

Let's touch on the basic meaning of each of these commandments before we get into the specific mechanics of our **PLAN**.

I. The first rule of making money is not to lose it.

There is no such animal as a get-rich-quick scheme. There are only get-poor-quick schemes. If an investment sounds too good to be true, it is. No one is going to share a secret way of making money that they could keep to themselves and continue to use to reap great profits. That fairy tale doesn't happen in the real world, so don't count on being the first (and only) person in recorded history to come across such a charitable individual. If you desire wealth, you will have to come by it the old-fashioned way. You must earn it. Slowly and deliberately by keeping your resources and allowing them to continually grow.

The Ultimate Ponzi Scheme Of Bernie Madoff

THE FINANCIER AND convicted felon Bernie Madoff estimated, by his own account, that he had stolen $50 billion in personal and institutional wealth from the rich people in Palm Beach, New York, Abu Dhabi, the French Riviera, London, and Spain as well as many other places. He was able to cross so many international borders to the rich and famous because there was a single denominator to his larceny. For almost thirty years, Madoff made the too-good-to-be-true seem like it was true. Greed and lack of oversight took over and did the rest of the work to promote his con. His Ponzi scheme had been done many times before, but never with such international flair.

The Madoff black hole of wealth was a classic "Ponzi scheme," named after a famous Boston swindler in 1920. Charles Ponzi went from being flat broke to having ten million dollars in six months. A Ponzi scheme works this way: cash gathered from new investors is used to pay off old investors. The returns look great, but they are all on paper. No earning is taking place: cash coming in one door goes out through the other door, and everyone is happy thinking they are earning solid returns. The "profit" that Madoff showed his investors on their statements wasn't worth the cost of printing the page.

Madoff claimed a proprietary investment system. Very few looked at the details. Instead they saw great returns on official-looking paper statements. Most of his investors continued to risk the "profits" instead of taking back their principal and profit amount. In some few cases the "profits" were used by older investors for living expenses, but most left their "profits" to continue to compound and grow their investment. There was plenty of money coming in to cover the few redemptions of cash going out. This allowed Madoff and a select few "feeders" to live a very lavish lifestyle. The feeders sent new financial lambs to the slaughter, and Madoff sheared their assets.

Madoff's sales technique created the impression that his funds were so good they were closed to new investors. But he had his agents travel all over the world telling potential victims that they might be able to get into a Madoff fund because the feeder had a direct relationship with him. The message was out that a Madoff account allowed you to join an exclusive club where you could make above-average returns easily and consistently. Looking at Madoff's list of rich and famous clients, you had to be impressed. How could such smart people be wrong? Investing with Madoff must be a privilege (they thought), since he claimed to produce steady and solid returns that exceeded the traditional financial markets every single year.

The problem, of course, was that nothing was growing in value. Madoff made no actual investments. A Ponzi scheme can go on as long as more cash comes in than goes out. The doom of the Madoff firm came with the general financial crisis of 2008, when many investors needed cash. Once people started taking out funds more quickly than Madoff could find fresh suckers to put in new cash, everything imploded. The people who begged Madoff to manage their life savings then begged him to return their investments. But there was no money to return. The statements that people received quarterly were just pieces of paper that could not be converted to real money.

II. Thou shalt not forget that money is only money and not character or fame.

The correct temperament for making and keeping money is an understanding that your life has many facets and wealth is only one of them. Having a job you like to go to and a family life beyond work is just as important a store of success as the dollars available in your investment accounts. Money tends to accrue to people who are well rounded and happy in all parts of their life.

III. Thou shalt honor experienced people who have money, and profit from their knowledge.

You can learn a great deal about investing by reading the experience of people such as Warren Buffet, Peter Lynch, Bill Miller, and a host of other successful investors. This material is easily located on the Internet or in bookstores and is often full of useful content. Time allocated to absorbing their thought process is well spent even though most people will not reach their level of wealth. It is also a good idea to associate with individuals in your own life who have had some financial success and are willing to discuss with you how they achieved it.

IV. Thou shalt not worship thy investment advisor, for if she were so smart she would be retired by now.

In general, most market analysts and financial reporters are experts who will know tomorrow why the things they predicted yesterday did not happen. If you expect to get rich quick on the back of some secret investment guru, all I have to say is, "Good luck to you, sport!" If you follow the latest trends blindly without your own analysis, you will eventually suffer financial collapse on the one hand and complete loss of your dreams on the other.

V. Many rogues swear falsely about secret opportunities, but only generating real profit is the chosen path to making money.

Making money is a deliberate process that involves hard work and restraint. If you absorb the material in this book, you can steer clear of schemes that are simply the latest get-rich-quick fads. Ignore the flashy guy at the tennis or golf club who tells you about his clever investment formula, which he cannot clearly explain because it's too complex. Dodge the pitch from a broker who is young and inexperienced. Don't fall for the TV shows that promise to make you a fortune in no-money-down real estate. The goal we have in mind for our **PLAN** is to get you to take evasive action when investing and focus on safety of your capital resources.

VI. Thy parents and relatives shall not be thy bankers.

There is added pressure in using money that your closest family members have worked hard to gain. In general, this is a poor idea that can have consequences for your emotional well being. Money from investors who understand risk and are prepared for it is a much better bet.

VII. Thou shalt not covet what thou art not willing to work for.

A recurring theme in the following pages is that managing and investing money is your second job regardless of what you do for a living. There is no shortcut.

VII. Thou shalt not swear at thy fate when things go badly but roll up thy sleeves and get back to work. (No one's listening anyway.)

Nothing takes the place of persistence and determination. You have to learn to trust yourself and your analysis of the facts. Failure in an investment is an opportunity to learn and improve for the next round. Others have achieved wealth and financial security and you can, too.

IX. Thou shalt not carry a credit card balance as this puts you in the devil's grasp.

Think of credit cards like the snake with the apple in the Garden of Eden. They seem like a very attractive and easy thing to use but improperly applied they will keep you out of the world of financial achievement.

X. Thou shalt not compromise principles just to reap a sum of money.

In the long run you will do best to stick by a well-thought-out **PLAN** rather than jump on board something that feels wrong but could be very profitable. Read the sidebar about the Madoff Ponzi scheme again and think about the sophisticated people who knew or felt there was something funny going on but got greedy. Levelheaded investing is a methodical process and should not be compromised by black-box gambling.

XI. Thou shalt avoid the false idols of the news and money press and follow thine own mind.

We live in an instant information age and sometimes there is too much of it. In our **PLAN** there are suggestions about using the more reliable financial press as opinion input. Common sense and a realistic appraisal of your skills and resources are most likely to lead to financial triumph. There is simply too much time in twenty-four hour news to fill it with a constant stream of quality information, so choose your sources carefully. Peter Lynch, one of the most successful investors of all time, used his common sense to produce very uncommon profits on his investments. If his family used and enjoyed a particular product, he reasoned that the company that made it was a good investment. Simple, but very effective, reasoning.

XII. Thou shalt not be afraid to risk thy money but be mindful of possible consequences if a loss ensues.

A core part of our safe and secure **PLAN** is to properly adjust risk in your financial life. Never "bet the ranch" on a single toss of the dice because starting over from scratch is a hard thing to do. Measure the downside of what you are attempting with great precision and be prepared for an outcome that is not what you expected.

XII. Money saved in store sales at the holidays is money thou hast earned.

Timing your purchase of everything from major consumer goods to stocks and bonds gives you a leg up on achievement. When you understand the situation of the moment you maximize the likelihood of a positive outcome in wealth creation. Waiting for sale seasons to buy a car or sound system stretches your buying power. What you can conserve you don't have to work for.

XIV. At life's end thy money shall not accompany thee onward.

Make your goal of financial stability a part of life but not the entire purpose of your life. You don't want to be the richest man in the cemetery.

XV. The closer thy life is to owning things outright without debt, the closer thou art to heavenly bliss.

The burden of debt is a crushing problem for many people. It causes them to be greedy and reach for investment returns that are unrealistic and probably unattainable. Our PLAN is not to gamble but to methodically work with available income, cash flow, and investing in such a way as to remove borrowing and liability as much as possible.

These commandments are pretty close to what anyone desiring to build wealth needs to think about. You will have to make up your own mind as to the path your financial life will take and apply each commandment for the benefit of you and your family unit. While there is effort and learning involved, the fact is it won't require consultation with a burning bush. Try out the PLAN for a few months and see how it functions within your life. You can change any aspect you wish to suit your particular circumstances. Whether you use this PLAN, an entirely different approach, or a hybrid of both, complete your education in this significant step toward wealth independence.

If you are careful and follow these commandments it should be possible to steer clear of the traps so many investors have fallen into. Think about the scandals that have harmed many investors in Ponzi schemes: one day you believe you are worth millions and feel very secure, and the next day you realize your net worth has evaporated. You have to start all over. If you are older and it was your retirement money, you have a bleak future ahead of you. If it was your child's college money, they may not be in school any longer. If you borrowed money to invest, you have lost everything on one side and still owe what you borrowed. That is a financial and mental hardship that you had better be prepared to face if you ignore these financial commandments.

No one beats the normal returns of the traditional financial market year in and year out. Sometimes you win; sometimes you lose. With an eye on these commandments and a PLAN similar to the one we will discuss, you will enhance the odds of affluence and prosperity during your lifetime.

2

MY STORY

My father was a child of the Great Depression that hit America and most of the rest of the world in the 1930s. It was a time in which wealth for most people consisted of having enough money to put food on the table and a roof overhead. He was a smart man who graduated high school near the top of his class, and he wanted to go to college. He was, in fact, accepted at Columbia University but the pressure to earn an income had to take precedence over continuing education. As the youngest of thirteen children living in a rambling old house in Yonkers, New York, he was expected to take whatever place could be found for him in the job market. It was a communal effort that kept the Lee family afloat during that dark period in American financial history.

But David Lee had a spark within him that was unique. When he could find no employment for wages, he decided to create his own job. I suppose today we would call him an entrepreneur. But it was a form of entrepreneurship that was born out of necessity and without formal training. He noticed that if he could purchase coal at a Pennsylvania mine and deliver it to the door of local housewives in Yonkers and the surrounding towns, there was a profit to be made. It is the most basic of business principles to buy in bulk at one price and sell at "retail" at another, higher, price.

He had no customers when he first started out so David Lee cold-called door-to-door and soon acquired a route of homes willing to pay for coal delivery. Thus was born ADLEE FUEL CO., which later went on to deliver both coal and oil with three secondhand trucks. It was successful enough to help his parents and siblings get through rough times and keep him employed in delivering product people wanted and needed.

My father never achieved great wealth from his career as an entrepreneur. His little company was capital constrained and lacked the ability to go beyond a small geography of customers. Nevertheless he always had some money and was never at the threshold of insolvency. The formula he used for wealth creation was a simple one. David Lee never spent any money unless he absolutely had to. He was like many Great Depression children in this trait. For them, when money was earned it was first saved and later spent only when necessity forced a portion of savings to slip away.

When he later married, and my sister and I came along, this flinty businessman's appreciation for not spending manifested itself everywhere. When my mother insisted on a washing machine, he got a used one from a Laundromat. A long series of battles ensued between my parents that mimicked the Hundred Years War between two royal French houses, finally yielding victory to my mother, who went to Sears and bought a modern washing machine for the family laundry.

My father and I used to play doubles tennis on the weekends. In the heat of one summer, we entered a local father and son tournament. After playing three sets against another family team, and winning, I had become quite hot and thirsty. I asked my father for fifty cents to buy a grape soda; he refused because there was a public water fountain nearby. It was not within his psyche to spend money for self-reward when there was a free alternative available. I was determined from that summer forward to find the path to become financially independent enough to both live well and give my own family financial security. My friends who have heard this story will tell you that my foregone grape soda was the starting point of my own career as a careful entrepreneur and investor. At my fiftieth birthday party several of them gave me a six-pack of grape soda! I knew there had to be a better path to building wealth than simply saving every penny earned and denying life's small pleasures. It was up to me to find my way. And there is such a **PLAN** in this book.

I mostly paid my way through eleven years of university. It was a combination of borrowing, scholarships, and working. Sometimes there was some begging involved. The end result was a BA cum laude from Lehigh University, an MBA from the Wharton School of Finance and Commerce at the University of Pennsylvania, and a Juris Doctor degree from Fordham University School of Law (which I attended at night while working in New York City). Over the years I have had the pleasure of authoring six other books, mostly technical, and numerous articles in the area of finance and investing.

While my father delivered coal and oil, my mother worked as a secretary, tended the home, and gardened. There was no real push toward higher education or a drive by them to accumulate meaningful wealth. I realized that education is the first building block of a **PLAN**. That revelation can be traced to some fine grade school teachers who pushed a few of their charges to break out from a marginal public school. I will be forever grateful to the librarian who forced me and another student in my class to read the collected fifty Great Books Series in the seventh and eighth grades, although I didn't tell her that at the time.

During high school summers I mowed many lawns to earn tuition money for college. Sweating in the summer sun in that entry-level outdoor job, I realized that the ingredient for changing my future was a medium called money. Lawn care is an honest job, but it was a far cry from the professional journey I wanted to undertake and a limiting field of endeavor. However, this physical labor was one of the many refueling stops necessary to reach my ultimate destination. As high school ended I reached a crossroads: accept more lawn customers for increased income; work as an employee in a landscape company; start a landscape company; or spend what I had earned on college to leave this gardening profession and begin another. It was very much a road trip—choose a route from the map and that determines where you will go and how quickly you will arrive.

In college I needed much more money than lawn work could provide, so I compromised my time with a few really awful jobs. There was a high wage for emptying the grease traps in restaurant kitchens in Bethlehem, Pennsylvania, because no one wanted to do it. It meant getting down in a grease pit in waist-high boots, scooping the fat and grease into a bucket, and emptying the tank. I was certain at that life intersection that graduate studies were in my endgame horizon and nothing else I could reasonably do paid as well. So the buckets of grease were really tickets to another fork in my journey. The task would be over soon, but the money benefit would move me down the road to a future I desired.

Later I landed a job in a local factory attaching the seatback buttons on couches as they slowly meandered along a snakelike assembly line. Each couch came with a swatch of material from which eighteen round tops had to be cut. After cutting the tops, I pressed them onto a button form on a compression machine. Next I threaded nine buttons on twelve-inch needles, pulled them through the couch, and tied each one to another button to hold the two in place. Boring? Yes, but warm and without the fumes of the grease traps. The pay was very good, and the other workers would allow me to ride around on couches and study during exam periods.

After undergraduate work I was accepted at the Wharton School of Finance at the University of Pennsylvania. This was my first formal training in business management techniques, but I still continued to earn and save. Another student and I opened a store inside an old school bus that sold candles, surplus military clothing, and supplies needed by other students. By then it was clear that in order to understand money and get a lifetime **PLAN** I had to go to Wall Street upon graduation. A major bank hired me as a trainee in bonds; later, I traded stocks. During the four years I spent in the New York financial world I learned that investing wisely meant limiting risk and not spending everything I had earned on current living expenses. If I simply pretended that my pay was about half of its actual amount, and invested the other half carefully, the compounding of money soon began to create wealth.

Wall Street was not my long-term goal so I decided to get into venture capital and move to the operating side of business creation. The venture funds where I worked or consulted have financed more than forty companies. Most of these started out as private investments although several became large publicly traded companies. I was never a passive investor and always paid attention to each investment and did my homework. I stuck to a **PLAN** for managing risk by also buying bonds to produce additional income and having only a relatively small stock market portfolio.

One of the health-care companies I cofounded and headed for thirteen years as president and later chairman and CEO started on a shoestring and grew from two people to seventeen hundred employees, with $400 million in annual medical-supply sales. It helped make the lives of millions of senior diabetics a little better by sending them necessary items via the mail. The company was eventually sold to a larger corporation after I retired for $1.5 billion. In another situation, I was one of three founders and investors in a fiber optic sensor company that started with five people and ended up six years later with 120 employees and $20 million in sales before it was sold to a large airplane manufacturer. Each time these investments were sold, the proceeds were not spent but reinvested once again in new opportunities.

My family has always lived quite well and we enjoy life but never forget to save. I do not share my father's extreme position about hoarding money, but at the same time we never invade our investment capital to stop its compounding growth. There are two kinds of money: one kind that you earn and spend and another that you earn and save. My hope is that the road map of *The Money Plan* will lead you on the same fantastic journey I have enjoyed. It can happen but there is work to be done, diligent care and attention to be paid, and persistence needed to move to your financial goal. If you understand and use the parts of the **PLAN**, I am confident in your ability to produce wealth and manage it correctly.

3

WHO YOU, THE READER, ARE

Everyone who invests can use a little sharpening up with alternative investment techniques and methodology. Our **PLAN** is a kind of fitness manual for your money. By this I mean that it should get you into better and better shape the longer you stick with it. In this respect the **PLAN** has something for everyone who will take the time to consider its elements. There is no single profile of those who can benefit the most from becoming familiar with interest rates, stock, bonds, budgeting, planning, cash flow, effective record-keeping, borrowing, and other topics relating to or involving money and finance. I suspect sharpening attention to these money subjects is good regardless of your age.

However, each generation has a discrete amount of lifetime remaining to invest and reap a reward. This book is a get-rich-slowly **PLAN**. The younger you are when you adopt the **PLAN** the more cumulative benefits it is likely to bring to you. We shall consider in a later chapter the topic of time passage and how it facilitates money compounding on itself to create wealth. I believe there are still meaningful benefits to Baby Boomers, Generation X, and Generation Y in the **PLAN**.

If you want to know what generational description fits consider these experiences?

- Howdy Doody and Buffalo Bob
- Mr. Ed and Wilber
- President Kennedy dies
- E.T.
- John Lennon dies
- 9/11

Howdy Doody was a frontier puppet program on live TV from 1947 to 1960, and Mr. Ed was the first talking horse, who debuted in a Filmways situation comedy in January 1961. If you knew the above then you are a "Baby Boomer" (born 1946-1964) and part of a population explosion that began with the cessation of hostilities in WWII. President Kennedy was assassinated in 1963, and E.T. from the Steven Spielbeg movie returned home in 1982. If you identify with these events, you belong to "Generation X" who were born between 1961 and 1981.

And if John Lennon from the Beatles being shot in New York in December 1980, and the New York and Washington, D.C., attacks on September 11, 2001, date you, then you are a "Generation Y" (also called "Echo Boomers") who were born between 1981 and 2004.

Baby Boomers as a group knew little about money and money management. After the war their parents' emphasis often was on family, country, or completing a college degree under the GI Bill. In general there was not a push to understand the financial markets as these matters were thought best handled by Wall Street. Bank savings accounts were widely regarded by Baby Boomers as a good thing. Our **PLAN** reinforces the value of saving but applies the funds in a more diverse way than bank instruments. The information in *The Money Plan* can be helpful for Baby Boomers because it provides some additional money principles to teach and discuss with their grandchildren.

"Generation X" really began the push for generating wealth and financial security. The introduction of the personal computer, with readily available financial Internet information, made individual investing possible. In addition, the widespread entry of women into the workforce increased household earnings, and some of these extra funds found their way into mutual funds, stocks, and real estate. The **PLAN** can help them clearly budget and target financial goals. One of these important milestones is investing for retirement.

Our **PLAN** should be especially useful to Generation Y as they have a long period of time to earn money and invest. They are the current young professionals with good educations, increasing incomes, and the most time to save and invest. Properly handled the compound effect of money during a long period should bring reasonable affluence.

Many readers of this book aspire to become a millionaire for the safety and lifestyle it embraces. Our **PLAN** can help construct certain guidelines that might make this realistic for Generation Y and perhaps for Generation X. A millionaire can be defined as a person or family unit whose net worth (the total value of all property owned) exceeds one million dollars in U.S. currency. However, inflation tends to decrease the value of a dollar in terms of its purchasing power. A million dollars in 1900 would be the equivalent of 24.8 million dollars in 2006 using the Consumer Price Index as a basis. (See the sidebar on top next page). The purchasing power of a million dollars in 1959 would be the same as 7.3 million dollars in 2009. So being a millionaire is relative depending on the external market events that transpire during your lifetime. In rough statistics, there are about ten million people in the world who are millionaires, with the largest number in the United States and second in Japan.

According to www.wealthvest.com/blog/tag/Alex-rodriguez (October 30, 2010) there is no single "correct" measure to compare relative value money comparisons over time. However, he points out that the Babe Ruth signed a contract in 1930 with the New York Yankees at an annual salary of $80,000. By 2009, the CPI was 14 times larger than it was in 1931 and that means that the Babe's purchasing power was the equivalent of about $1,000,000 salary today. Using other methods than the CPI it would be even higher. For example, using GDP per capita Babe Ruth's earnings relative to average output would be $6,000,000 today.

HOW MUCH MONEY DO I NEED TO EARN?

The natural question to ask is, "How much money do I need to earn?" It is a little like asking a five-year-old how much candy he wants to eat on Halloween night. He wants to eat as much as he can without getting sick. You should probably want to earn as much as you can, while having a great life, and not ending up as the youngest millionaire in the graveyard. However, if you study hard, work hard, have a little luck, invest carefully, and stick to a **Plan**, there is a good chance you can become part of the U.S. population who are millionaires.

Our discussion wouldn't be complete if we didn't have a general guideline for all generations comparing income and assessing what it means in terms of relative wealth. When you first enter the work force a multiplier of 2.0 to 3.0 times your age puts you at an excellent starting point. Earning power (and savings ability) should grow from there. Clearly, the first several levels of income in Chart 3.1 are to cover the elements of a basic middle class family budget. Your most lofty future goals—such as two or more houses, an around-the-world trip, owning a prestigious car and private plane, or collecting fine antiques—are good, but unless you make a monthly income in the last three categories of the table below, you may have to prune these types of items from your wish list.

The table is a rough chart that certain financial planners use of levels of income to determine relative earning success. Keep in mind that the U.S. Census shows an income of $100,000 per year puts you in the top 20% of all households. When you earn more it is possible to invest more and when it is done carefully over time the growth in financial assets can make you wealthy. Examine it to assess your standing against a probable peer group level of success, but don't think it is an absolute. At any stage changed circumstances such as starting a new business that expands rapidly can jump you several categories.

– CHART 3.1 –
MONTHLY INCOME (1)

	INCOME	WHAT IT MEANS FOR WEALTH GOAL
Level 1	$5-7,000	Good start (2)
Level 2	$8-10,000	Getting there
Level 3	$11-13,000	You made it
Level 4	$14-16,000	Possible millionaire
Level 5	$17,000 or more	Millionaire wealth

(1) Not taking tax burden into account.
(2) For those below 30 years old.

PRESENT AND FUTURE VALUE CONCEPTS

MONEY IS A numbers game. You may wish to dust off your old textbooks or review college notes about the rudimentary basics of accounting and finance. This background would be somewhat helpful but not critical. Our PLAN is easier to understand. We are aiming at nothing too fancy: it's like driving a car. You shouldn't get behind the wheel unless you can steer. It's just not safe. And it is not safe to invest without mastering some basic concepts. The starting point is the three possible courses of action when you are in receipt of money:

    a. You can receive money now and spend it now. If you do, that money will not be invested and grow over time.

    b. You can expect to receive money at some future date. Since you can't spend the money for a long time, it is worth less to you than if you could buy something with it today. But if you want some part of the money today, you must locate an institution or individual willing to wait for the future sum who will pay you a lesser amount today, for their inconvenience of the postponed receipt of the full amount. You may be content with the smaller amount because it is spendable now in the present moment.

    c. You can receive money now but not spend it now. Instead, the money may be invested until some future date. When you finally get the money plus its earnings, the total amount will be larger than the original sum you received.

Would you rather have $5,000 today or receive it in ten years? Clearly, common sense tells us that you will instinctively say you want the $5,000 immediately. You can spend or invest the money for ten years if you have it now. Possibility "**a**" above is over and done with at once. The spent money has neither present nor future value because it went into an electronic gadget only a twelve-year-old nerd can work. With Possibility "**b**," money in the future has a current value but that value is logically less than the total paid later. Possibility "**c**" gets you the money now, but you don't want to spend it so you sock it away for a later expenditure. The money will earn a return and thus have a greater later value. So what do we call these events, and how do we calculate the actions from possibilities "**b**" and "**c**"?

Present value is the terminology for the $5,000 that someone will give you in ten years. It is plainly not worth the same amount as $5,000 in your hands today because you can't spend or invest it until you actually receive it ten years from now. The present value of the $5,000 received ten years in the future is undoubtedly some fraction less than $5,000 received today. Hold on to that thought.

Now let's look at the other side of that coin. **Future value** begins if you have money in your hand today that can be invested for a period of years. As long as we don't lose the **principal** (the starting amount), the earnings on that money will build up and give us more money back ten years in the future. It will be the principal plus all of the earnings that are added to it. So the future value of $5,000 received today and invested for ten years is far greater than $5,000, depending on the rate of return received each year and added to the principal. The *rate of return* is the earnings expressed as a percentage. For example, a certificate of deposit at a bank for one year with 3.5 percent interest is a rate of return for that year of 3.5 percent. A stock market gain in a year of 7 percent is a 7 percent rate of return. And so on.

Now let's find out how we determine how much more or less our $5,000 is worth over ten years. Everything depends on how high a rate of return our money can produce in each individual year during the time period. This is called the *time value of money*. One year we may invest in a certificate of deposit; the next year in stocks; another year in a business; and another year in a bond. It is all about your overall average rate of earnings during the time period. In this case the investment goes on for ten years. For simplicity, we will choose a constant rate of return for all ten years that reflects a very conservative investing style. If we always bought a ten-year bond that paid 6 percent interest each year, then the interest payment on the bond would be our yearly return to plug into the future value calculator.

OK, let's do some calculations. It's not important to know the formulas for calculating the present value or future value of money. There are automatic calculators readily available on the Internet. You can also use an inexpensive hand-held calculator. However, I will put the formulas here for the folks who are not challenged by math:

$$\text{Present Value} = \text{Future Value} \times (1 + i)^{-n}$$
$$\text{Future Value} = \text{Original sum} \times (1 + i)^{n}$$

"i" is the interest rate per period

"n" is the number of periods

Let's just plug into these equations our $5,000 that will be given to us in ten years and see what its **present value** would be if the interest rate each period for ten years is 6 percent. The answer is that it is worth only $2,791.97 today. Now for the flip side, look at *future value*. Let's plug in our $5,000 given to us today and see what its future value is worth in ten years at the same 6 percent interest rate. The answer is that it is worth $8,954.24 in ten years.

Once again, you don't need to work the equations. Just go to Google or Bing and search for *"present value calculator"* or *"future value calculator"*—there are numerous free programs to perform the math. Simply plug in the numbers in the right places and click "calculate." These two calculations above took less than thirty seconds to obtain and complete.

Don't fail to get started because you are thinking this is all too difficult. It's not. You can't know how much you have to save today for a major expenditure like your child's first year of college without doing the math. The Internet will make this relatively easy as we shall demonstrate in later chapters.

YOUR CHILD GOES TO COLLEGE

It is generally a safe bet to assume your children will enter college at age eighteen and be there at least four years. That should be part of your PLAN. The first step is to decide on the type of college (public or private) you would like for your kids to attend and calculate the future value of today's tuition cost using a moderate inflation rate as your interest rate. So let's do that.

Let's say that today the tuition at a private university of the type you hope your child will attend is $25,000 per year including room and board. The child in question is four years old, so you have fourteen years to save. You will have to make a few assumptions. First, assume that tuition increases will only match inflation. Second, assume your child wants to go to college. Third, assume that he/she has the grades to be accepted at the university. If you assume an inflation rate of 2.5 percent in this fourteen-year period, that is what you use in your future value calculator to estimate his/her first year's tuition.

As an exercise in future value let's see how much the tuition per year is likely to cost in fourteen years on our assumption of a 2.5 percent yearly inflation. Go to the Internet and pick a site with a free *future value* calculator. The future value of $25,000 at an inflation rate of 2.5 percent for a period of fourteen years is easy to calculate. Fill in the numbers on your Internet calculator to conclude that today's $25,000 tuition will cost approximately $35,465 per year in fourteen years. It is probably close enough to multiply this number by four to give an approximate total cost of $142,000 for your first child to complete a four-year undergraduate degree. (This number will appear as a future goal in the Whipped Cream and Cherry Budget we discuss later.)

Now let's make it a more exact number and figure out the annual contribution needed to get there. The Financial Industry Regulatory Authority (FINRA) is the largest independent regulator for all securities firms doing business in the United States. FINRA's mission is to protect America's investors by making sure the securities industry operates fairly and honestly. You can trust the information from their Web site. Go to Google and enter, "FINRA college claculator," and input annual college cost today, years until enrollment, annual return on investments, number of years the child will be enrolled, and inflation rate. The calculator will provide an annual contribution rate needed to reach your future goal. In addition, the FINRA site has a publication entitled College Savings Plan Options, which provides more information and guidance.

You will want to calculate this future goal several times for various inflation rates, types of colleges, and return on investments. As always, it pays to be conservative and follow our philosophy of safe and secure. Don't assume an extreme rate of return that makes your numbers look good but leaves reality behind when you actually get to the future and have to pay. Included below is a chart from the FINRA Web site with some information on college pricing trends based on 2009 information.

AVERAGE COST OF FOUR YEARS OF COLLEGE

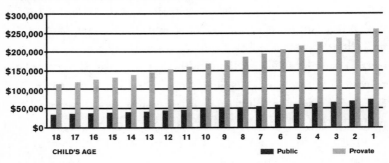

Source: *Trends in College Pricing 2009*, The College Board®. Assumes a 5 percent increase in college costs each year and a child entering college at age eighteen.

Your financial planning job over the next fourteen years will be to decide on the combination of savings, scholarships, and loans that will enable you to meet this major expense. It may seem daunting, but with good planning lots of families get through it. If you have children who will overlap in college, you must allow for the multiple tuitions in each year of their overlap. Obviously college is one of the larger financial goals and may actually be equal to the expenses involved in the purchase of a new home.

4

YOU CAN BE WEALTHY IF YOU HAVE A PLAN

"Money is better than poverty if only for financial reasons."
–WOODY ALLEN

Having money is better than not having it, but the quest for money should not consume your life. The truth is the best way to not have to constantly think about money is to have a lot of it. You can reasonably expect to become well off financially if you follow a long-term **PLAN** and apply your income wisely. A good **PLAN** for getting prosperous works within specific boundaries; you must put it in motion and stick with its core principles. Adopting the culture of the **PLAN** in this book means understanding its core values and how they are important:

CORE CULTURE MAXIMS

- If you want to be wealthy you have to think about saving as well as getting.
- Let money do the work. The miracle of compounding can work day and night so you don't have to.
- Never spend money before you have it.
- Most people don't take care of their money until they have run out of it. (Other people do the same thing with their time.)

- It is just as difficult to manage money as to obtain it.
- The use of money is the main advantage in having money.

Our **PLAN** requires a good deal of effort, discipline, and time to become wealthy. That is the cost for achieving financial success. It is always "something for something" in the world of finance. Maintaining your **PLAN** is a second job that in many ways is as important as your primary one.

There are gambles on Wall Street that sometimes pay off, but more often than not the risk is a path of unfulfilled promises for the "little folks." Much conventional money wisdom suggests gaining riches by investing aggressively in equity instruments, such as stocks, and using leverage to increase your investable base. There are a few winners who have achieved extraordinary wealth that way, but many more individuals have seen their hard-earned-savings fail to grow or disappear altogether.

In the decade before this book was written, there were three meltdowns in the stock market. Those who placed the bulk of their assets in stocks have largely come away bloodied and without reward. Hopefully they have time to recover. After ten years the market return was at best about a break-even. That result translates into ten years of lost opportunity where the miracle of compounding never happened. Their stock portfolios remained stagnant or shrank. Income instruments, such as bonds and certain funds, however, generally continued to produce profits and cash flow for their owners.

Our **PLAN** uses the stock market and other equity instruments as a measured part of a portfolio. It does not avoid them entirely. But there is a bias toward income-generating investments such as bonds, dividend stocks, preferred shares, and other cash-producing mutual funds or exchange-traded funds (ETFs). The **PLAN** forgoes the quick return for a more methodical march to specific goals. It requires you to reflect on defined family needs and expectations. You might call it "the average person's path to wealth and security" versus the high flier's road, with its numerous dead ends. Even if you become quite sophisticated in your portfolio profile, the core of your actions can still remain within the fundamentals of our PLAN. You can choose to take more risk then if you like, but think of it as going to Las Vegas with a set amount of money to gamble. The rest stays in your pocket to be sure you can pay the fare back home.

QUID PRO QUO

The instruction in our methodology provides a fairly good grasp of some of the basic financial concepts and hopefully reduces them into a practical system. I have left out much of the unnecessary financial jargon and complex subjects that do not pertain to non-professional investors. That sort of material is covered in finance textbooks but is too theoretical to apply to the average person's money. Instead we have focused our efforts on the core components that usually work well—although there is no assured specific outcome in saving and investing. Some financial planners might disagree with my asset allocations, the benefit or risk in borrowing, or the emphasis on safe and secure management of risk. But just as many experts will agree that there is some merit there. You will have to decide if our PLAN makes you comfortable.

Here is an overview of the steps that make up the whole of the PLAN that you will discover in the following pages:

THE MONEY PLAN

1. Establish a *rainy-day fund*.
2. Pay off all *credit card debt* and pay balances monthly.
3. Regard *borrowing and leverage* with skepticism.

4. Work on constantly increasing your *cash flow*.

5. *Save 20-50 percent* of earned income.

6. Invest using *dollar-cost averaging*.

7. *Diversify* as the key to a safe and secure financial life.

8. Rely on *bonds* as the basis of a reduced-risk investing strategy—they can work as well as stocks.

9. Recognize the risk of *stocks* if you decide to include them in your portfolio.

10. Investigate *ETFs* and *SPDRs* as useful tools.

11. Be careful and willing to work hard if you decide to invest in *real estate*.

12. Set up digital and hard-copy *record-keeping systems* with offsite backup.

13. Construct a *Worksheet* from receipts.

14. Fill in a *Ham-and-Egg Budget* with your baseline items for the year.

15. Use *future value* to determine how inflation will affect any goal-line items that are more than five years away.

16. Fill in a *Whipped-Cream-and-Cherry Budget* with your goal-line items.

17. Construct and date a *Personal Net Worth statement* as a personal balance sheet.

18. Read some publications such as *The Wall Street Journal*, *Forbes*, *Bloomberg Business Week*, *Barron's* and *Kiplinger's Personal Finance*. They can all be had online although a hard-copy subscription will allow you to build a readily accessible library.

IT'S YOU, BABY...IT'S YOU

Unless you are planning to have the tooth fairy place several million dollars under your pillow, it is important to know as much about your money as possible. We are assuming that you desire financial security for yourself and your family. In order to provide it, you and your spouse need to take direct control of your present financial situation and make the future happen with a **PLAN**. Please remember the words "you" and "**PLAN**." There is no one else who can be entrusted with this task. Not Mom or Dad. Not your broker, financial planner, or insurance agent. Not your good pal who looks so successful when you see him at the country club. The list of "nots" is endless. Let's begin the process.

YOUR FINANCIAL THREE-LEGGED STOOL

What follows in the pages of this book is a macro view of a **PLAN** to guide you through the major monetary decisions of life. It's a three-legged stool on which you can securely rest. A one- or two-leg stool is wobbly and not firm underneath you. But with three legs your position is secure and steady. Similarly our **PLAN** has three legs of support for your financial well-being.

1. *A safe and secure approach* is our first leg. Those are our watchwords: "safe and secure." They have a central place in any intelligent financial plan. It is a basic supporting leg of our **PLAN** that your family move in a careful and deliberate way to economic independence.
2. *The consistent increase of available cash flow* is the second leg of our stool.
3. *Careful and educated investment execution* is the third leg.

All three of the above together make our three-legged stool sturdy. Take away any one and the **PLAN** may wobble or not work.

The **PLAN** is proactive and you and your family have to employ it to save, invest, guard, and spend the money earned in your lifetime. Because you make up the budgets and set the priorities, the end result is very personal to your own family and its finances. There is some instruction on specific topics but it is not intended to be a complete overview of the thousands of different components and economic mysteries of personal finance. Nor is it a ponderous reference work designed to transform you into a financial market guru. The intent of our **PLAN** is quite the opposite. We are going to cover some basics on how to manage and grow capital from any starting level with a practical **PLAN**.

There are no guarantees in the competitive world of wealth acquisition. Everyone is trying to earn their own piece of a finite pie of affluence. In business school, exams require the answer to a financial problem to be an exact number. Planning is a little different. When we do math in our plan, we are mostly looking for an approximate target. Planning is a look from five thousand feet up rather than an exact distance measured on the ground. It is my belief that people ignore this type of calculation at their continued peril. They will check the change from a cashier, argue about a slight discrepancy on a water bill, become enraged at not getting the lowest sale price on an item, but do not perform the slightest amount of homework to figure out how much they must save to send their kids to college.

Your formal education is important in helping you make a good living. But more important is your self-education in matters of finance. Money buys your ticket of mobility in work and play. As Ayn Rand said, "Money is only a tool. It will take you wherever you wish, but it will not replace you as the driver."

5

PLANNING

My wife says that I am the most organized person she knows. I stand guilty as charged. However, in my experience within the business and financial worlds there has never been a successful CEO or investor who did not have a detailed organizational system. When things went wrong, they could fall back on the records and find the problem to be corrected. Locating the problem quickly was more than half the battle.

If you don't know where you have been financially, you cannot possibly know where you are going. Being on top of the data in our digital era is power and control for your **PLAN**. Planning is a method for achieving an objective through arrangements that are made in advance. For individuals, good record-keeping systems are often the biggest challenge. Perhaps it is because we believe that the creative side of our lives is not cultivated with bean counting. Maybe we are just lazy. Then there is the fact that it is time consuming and tedious to constantly upgrade information in a useful fashion.

Let's be succinct here and state why record-keeping is so important. If you want to get into the big show, you need to know where you are headed. It's our **PLAN** that focuses you to do that. The **PLAN** tracks your progress toward your goals and provides the concrete information used to make decisions along the way. The basics of our **PLAN** information system are:

1. It must have a baseline starting point.
2. It must be understandable.
3. It must be easy to use.
4. It must be reliable.
5. It must be timely.

1. RECORD-KEEPING

IT'S ALL COMING FROM THE RECORD-KEEPING SYSTEM

As with most things that work, the system proposed here is remarkably simple and based on common sense. Our system of tracking is most decidedly in agreement with Thomas Jefferson when he said, "I can never fear that things will go far wrong where common sense has fair play." Common sense dictates we know what we own, what price we own it at, and how it is performing in increasing our wealth.

We're not dealing with rocket science in our system, and yet I am continually amazed at how disorganized most people are in their personal finances. Professionals who run an office or company like clockwork fail to apply even a fraction of the same effort to their private portfolios. If you join their ranks you may live just fine on your considerable income, but you are unlikely to become wealthy. Accurate record-keeping enables better decision making, which leads to success. While you may tailor parts of this commonsense approach to fit your unique needs, most of it is important—overlook the details at your peril.

Virtually every successful company in the world has a sophisticated computer system and backs up this digital form of data on its servers along with physical paper records. When you go to a doctor's office, records may be available digitally, but in the exam room there is almost always a handwritten patient file as well. These two methods are a time-tested combination that provide a measure of security in a computerized world that still has a fair amount of lost and misplaced data. Why would we approach a system for wealth accumulation in any other manner? We are going to adopt the same basic concept: the best available digital software backed up by two commonsense paper filing systems and a remote data backup. I will try to provide you with a rough idea of the time needed for each part, but it will ultimately depend on your basic familiarity with computers and finance. Our method is in concert with our principle of safe and secure. The four parts of the system are digital records, paper investment files, a paper receipt file, and an offsite storage company.

1. DIGITAL RECORDS

Records of investments, performance, checking, electronic fund transfers (EFTs), portfolios, brokerage accounts, mutual funds, net worth, budgets, and anything financial in digital form may be kept in *Quicken*® software. I have seen all the available software, and Quicken is the clear winner. You can learn its basics in a day. There are three versions of this software, but for our purposes *Quicken Premier Version* is the most useful. This inexpensive product is available from the Intuit Company at www.Quicken.com or from any store that sells a decent selection of software. It's a good idea to update your Quicken software yearly.

Each month as you balance your checkbook and reconcile *electronic fund transfers* (monthly direct payments from your bank to a vendor) and *ARC* checks (onetime transaction draws by a vendor), assign a category to every payment. Quicken will remember the payer and the category. This is an easy way to build the data bank for your worksheet. It is also the best way to get a real handle on your flow of funds so you never have a negative balance or a returned check.

Quicken will also enable you to download statement information directly from certain financial institutions (Fidelity, Vanguard, your bank, most brokerage firms) into its program, making monthly reconciliation even easier. However, you should still insist on receiving a mailed hard copy of statements. On at least a dozen occasions I have discovered major errors in digital financial records that could have cost thousands of dollars. In one case the error was $100,000 that was "lost" in the digital system. Perhaps it would have shown up by year end, but I don't want to take such chances. The only way to prove there was an error of that magnitude was with hard copies of checks that were deposited and statements of the history of the account. Some large institutions, especially major banks, are particularly error prone.

There is no shortcut around the Quicken Premier step in our **PLAN**. The sooner you start using this software, the easier it will be. As your portfolio and budgets get more and more complex with increasing wealth and responsibility, digital records are a necessity. Bite the bullet now, put in the time, and just do it.

Getting your records into a Quicken database is the hardest step in our record-keeping system, but you have to learn Quicken only once. The software comes with reasonable beginner instructions, and the "Quicken Help" function is easy to use. It takes about half a day for the basics and then you can learn more as you use it. Thereafter, all you need is an online monthly electronic update (where available) or input from a monthly paper statement. Adding the monthly statement information from your broker, bank, and other financial sources only takes about two to three hours of work per month to complete.

2. PAPER INVESTMENT FILES

It's true we are in the Internet world and paper records are not in vogue. Still, there is something very useful in hard-copy financial records. Buy a box of hanging and manila files. Clear out a file drawer. For every account you have at a financial institution, keep a separate hanging file folder in your financial file drawer. In each file folder include a copy of the papers you used to set up the account (never remove them in case you need to refer to them years later) as well as each month's statements during the year.

In addition, in front of your monthly investment account statements, keep the *confirmations* of any buy transactions in stocks and bonds for future reference to match up when you sell the investment. Clip them together for an easy record of what you bought, the date you bought it, and the price you paid. After you sell the investment, staple the buy and the sell paper confirmations together and transfer them to the *gain/loss records folder* you need for computing capital gains and losses each year. This information is sometimes on the monthly statements, but your saved confirmations are backup proof. At year end each institution is supposed to send you a summary statement of all trades during the year. It would be difficult to count the number of times over the years the statements had an error compared with my saved confirmations. Should you elect to have confirmations e-mailed to you, print them out and put them into the gain/loss records folder.

If you have twenty accounts, your financial file drawer will give you an easy visual scan of your portfolio diversification. It is also handy if you are unexpectedly incapacitated and someone else has to figure out what you have been doing. This is an excellent insurance continuity plan for you and your family.

This simple paper record-keeping system requires only an hour or two of filing time per month. At year end, when you're ready to prepare your tax returns, reach in each file and take out the twelve monthly statements, copy them, and send them to your tax accountant. Keep the originals in a box that holds records for each tax year in case you need them for an audit and you have changed accountants.

Why would I ever have twenty or more accounts?

You and your spouse may each have a money market account, separate self-directed IRAs, three or four special-purpose accounts (college accounts, home-purchase portfolio), a checking account, a savings account for each child to use to learn about money, a trust account, insurance policies, four or five mutual fund accounts, one or two brokerage accounts, and individual investments in owned real estate. It's not difficult to get to twenty or more folders.

▶ YOUR HOME HAS A SPECIAL FILE

When you sell your home, the basis of the purchase price you paid, plus all the improvements, are subtracted from the sales price to determine what tax, if any, you might owe. In your financial drawer there should be a "Home" file with all the closing documents from your purchase along with every receipt for the improvements you made over the years. If you have a large profit when you sell your home, having these helpful receipts from many years of ownership all in one place can save a lot of money and aggravation. It's simple, but most people are not disciplined enough to just throw receipts into the file and forget about them until they sell. If you want to get fancy, make a running list of all improvements and their cost and use this information to raise your cost basis and thus reduce the profit on which you might owe federal and state tax.

3. PAPER RECEIPT FILE

In a large expandable folder, sort and save every major retailer's sales receipts plus their statements. Also include the monthly statements from each credit card or charge card. Get in the habit of clipping together all the receipts from each retailer—that makes it easy to find a particular one several months later when you want to return something. In addition, keep all your utility bills, phone bills, mortgage receipts, property tax bills, and other bills clipped together. At the end of the year it will be easy to fill in your worksheet by adding up the yearly total. There is no work involved if the file is always in the same place and you transfer papers into it on the date of purchase or statement receipt. Make it a habit for yourself and other family members.

If you are starting your record-keeping system mid-year, just begin and continue to the end of the year. Then prorate what you have as totals to estimate a full year of purchases for use in the budget. If you start in July, by December you will have six months of records. By multiplying by two, you'll get a pretty good approximation of what the full twelve months might look like.

4. SAFEGUARDING DATA FROM LOSS

It seems like just about everyone has a major computer problem at one time or other. When a major loss occurs after, say, five years of record-keeping in Quicken, our paper backup is some comfort but reentering the data is tedious and difficult. It is a simple matter to sign up with one of the companies that store your data each day securely on their servers and can retrieve it to reload your computer or a new one. I particularly like www.carbonite.com and www.mozy.com but there are many others that perform this task for a modest annual fee. I use this in addition to a large external hard drive in my home so I feel completely safe in having access to my twenty-plus years of records.

This commonsense record-keeping system is so simple that I am amazed everyone doesn't use it. It is important that you not be lazy or fall prey to bad habits. The reason this system is so powerful is that it creates a *database* from which you will construct worksheets, make investments, prepare budgets, and do financial planning.

DOCUMENT IT ALL

Incapacity and death are part of life. Exit on a positive note without stressing everyone you left behind. As Garrison Keillor said, "They say such nice things about people at their funerals that it makes me sad that I'm going to miss mine by just a few days."

No one can make a flawless guess about all your wishes and carefully formulated plans. When individuals leave matters to oral history, there is certain to be disappointment, hurt, wasted resources, unnecessary delays, and a complicated labyrinth of problems. If your family is following some or perhaps all of our PLAN and has managed to achieve a measure of wealth, put some basic things in writing. There is no such thing as a perfect human recollection of what should be happening according to the wishes of an individual who can no longer reason and relate due to illness. Only instructions in black and white constitute a perfect communication and provide a call to action.

Almost all of the estate situations for which I have been consulted have demonstrated that for most people written documentation is woefully lacking. The common excuses are that there was no time, they couldn't locate a lawyer, they can't find the documentation, and their files needed to be put in order. Neither probate judges nor teachers accept the excuse that the dog ate the needed pages. The precise time that everyone must have this documentation inevitably coincides with an inability to gather it from an incompetent loved one. Once you are deceased or incapacitated, it is too late to record wishes, and the legal problems will commence. So here are the basic documents that should be in your family records:

1. *Will.*
2. *Durable power of attorney:* This document empowers your spouse or other trusted individual to collect, receive, and spend money on your behalf. It also has a host of other provisions to hire, discharge, represent, borrow, act in business, manage, join, and exercise power as though you were present.
3. *Designation of health-care surrogate:* Appoint an individual to make health-care decisions for you if you are incapacitated.
4. *Living will:* If you do not fear death as much as the indignity, deterioration, dependence, and hopeless pain

associated with an end-stage medical condition, you need a living will. It instructs your caregivers not to prolong a comatose state. It also specifies any anatomical gifts you wish to make to organ banks.

5. *Declaration naming a preneed guardian:* This short document selects people to be your guardian if your spouse is unable or somehow incapacitated.

It is a good idea to put these documents in a safe deposit box. Include trust documents, insurance papers, mortgages, deeds, and other important papers. However, you should maintain a *copy* of these originals in your home because they may be needed quickly. In most death situations the safe deposit box will be sealed for a time and your surviving family will have to act on your wishes before access can be accomplished.

WHEN "YOU" IS NOT YOU

IDENTITY THEFT **HAS** become a very big business. If you have become successful, chances are someone is going to attempt to hijack your good name to scam merchants. Many people find out their identity has been stolen when they apply for a store credit card and are told their credit is not acceptable because they skipped out on several accounts and have made far too many applications for other credit cards. Meanwhile, if you follow our PLAN, you know that you have never carried a balance or defaulted on a purchase. It means that your information is in the hands of thieves.

How did they get the information? Many times they pose as a legitimate Web site and ask you to respond to some questions. Other times they wait behind you in line and take a picture with their cell phone of your open wallet. Hackers also break into the databases of stores and financial institutions to steal massive amounts of data. It is even common for thieves to look through your garbage for statements and other information.

Take this threat to your wealth seriously and don't put any personal information on the Web unless it is safely encoded. Rarely give out your Social Security number, and then only to a legitimate bank or major institution whose privacy policy will protect it. Use a shredder for anything that contains sensitive information.

Lastly and most importantly, go to www.equifax.com, www.experian.com, and www.transunion.com once a year to get your free credit report. Note any unknown charges or applications and aggressively contest them in writing to remove them. Then follow up with each and every merchant to clear your name and report the fraud. You are entitled to demand a copy of the application they accepted at the time the account was opened. The real-world effect of not acting to set the record straight can be devastating.

Never, ever settle with a collection agency because you feel it is easier than fighting a false claim. Even though you are innocent, settling will severely affect your credit reports for many years. In the worst case, hire an attorney. It is money well spent.

2. BUDGETING

THE HAM-AND-EGG BUDGET

For our **PLAN** we are going to develop two different kinds of budgets. The *Ham-and-Egg Budget* sets your *baseline* on expenditures needed to maintain a living standard on income received in that year. It does not include any investment income, whether capital gains or ordinary income, from your portfolios. That is because you do not wish to spend this money but rather let it continue to compound and grow.

The *Whipped-Cream-and-Cherry Budget* sets your *goal line* and includes income from every source as well as your wish list of future use of that income. This is not a budget from which you will allocate spending but rather a budget that looks beyond the current year to provide for future financial events. These are expenditures such as buying a home or remodeling one, sending a child to college, planning for retirement income, and many other lifetime events that are personal to your family.

You begin this process by filling in a worksheet, which provides source data for these two budgets. The worksheet is the total picture of what you actually earn and spend. It is financial history and also reality. You will probably not fill in each line in the sample I provide below but will enter the information pertinent to your family's situation. The two budgets are where you want to direct your money flows in the coming year and beyond. I will admit that the first time you do this exercise, it is time consuming and confusing. It's no different from the initial frustration of learning to use a computer (or continually learning to play golf). However, the next time you do it the process will be much easier. Stick with it and you will gain a lot of control over your financial life.

Quicken Premier can be very useful for establishing your base-line Ham-and-Egg Budget if you have regularly input the necessary information into its Quicken Data (QDATA) databank. As you write checks, transfer funds electronically, and otherwise spend each month, assign a category to every expenditure in Quicken. It is best not to be too detailed as macro data works quite well for budget purposes. For example, if you own two cars, it isn't necessary to break out insurance, gas, and repairs for each vehicle. If you have a category called "clothing," lump together all your expenditures for the family rather than break them out by family member. The detail of each member's clothing expense will change from year to year, and we are only trying to obtain a gross number that can be budgeted.

Your Ham-and-Egg Budget is intended to map the basic inflows and outflows of your family's money in the coming year. In effect it is a bare-bones look at the minimum level needed to maintain your standard of living. There is no provision in the Ham-and-Egg Budget for using investment income for either monthly or extraordinary expense items.

The reason you create the Ham-and-Egg Budget in your **PLAN** is to have a starting point of reference. With every new event, such as the birth of a child, you can review the previous year's Ham-and-Egg Budget and compare it to the one for the coming year. This comparison will reveal areas in which expenses have significantly increased and allow you to evaluate them. Our method is not much different from what a public company does each quarter when it compares its current financial statement to last year's statement for the same quarter to determine the management plan for the coming year. It is often possible to reduce some unnecessary expenses without affecting your family's quality of life. You may be able to totally eliminate some of your expenses. But if you don't have two points of reference, how will you compare and know?

Your Ham-and-Egg Budget can also provoke you to rethink where to place expenses when you see a particular item jump dramatically as a percentage of your total budget. If your family has several teenagers who have begun to drive, it may be time to shop around for insurance companies rather than simply adding the new drivers to the policy you have had for many years. Think: "My Ham-and-Egg Budget gives me a road map for control over how I spend earned income."

It is also significant to review the possibilities for income expansion as part of the total budget equation. The greatest impact on income comes from a parent taking a second outside job, creating a second job in a home-based business, or a spouse returning to the workforce. The adults will have to balance the effort of doing more work against the desirability of major increases in the current year's expenses in the Ham-and-Egg Budget.

The first step toward creating a Ham-and-Egg Budget is to fill in the worksheets in *Chart 5.1* and *Chart 5.2* that list all types of income and expenses. In the second step, creating an actual budget, you will assign a characterization to each expense in *Chart 5.2* (that's what the **F, V, O, C** column is for). Using these two charts you can complete the process even if you hate your computer and don't know how to use Excel (a Microsoft financial software that creates tabulated spreadsheets). Quicken also has a budget function and can total many of the expense categories for you. I like to do it from my source paper file and records as that fixes many items in my mind and reveals relationships that might have otherwise been missed.

– **CHART 5.1** –
YEARLY INCOME WORKSHEET ITEMS
(As of   /   /   )

YEARLY AND MONTHLY INCOME BY SOURCE	YEARLY INCOME	MONTHLY INCOME	% OF TOTAL INCOME
1. Bond interest			
a. Corporate			
b. Municipal			
c. Zero-coupon			
d. Other			
2. Investment income			
a. Stocks			
b. Money markets			
c. Mutual fund distributions			
d. Checking interest			
e. Savings accounts			
f. Partnership income			
g. Other			
3. Additional income			
a. Alimony			
b. Child support			
c. Partnership income/loss			
d. Trust income			
e. Social Security Medicare			
f. Other			
4. Real Estate Income			
a. Mortgages			
b. Sole ownership			
c. REITs			

YEARLY AND MONTHLY INCOME BY SOURCE	YEARLY INCOME	MONTHLY INCOME	% OF TOTAL INCOME
d. Vacation home rental			
e. Other			
5. Earned income (gross before taxes)			
a. Primary earner			
b. Second earner			
c. Part-time occupation(s)			
6. Misc sources of income			
a.			
b.			
TOTAL INCOME			

– CHART 5.2 –
EXPENSE WORKSHEET ITEMS
(As of   /   /   )

YEARLY AND MONTHLY EXPENSES	YEARLY EXPENSE	MONTHLY EXPENSE	% OF TOTAL EXPENSE	F,V,O,C
1. Automobile				
a. Gas				
b. Repairs				
c. Insurance				
d. Commuting costs				
e. Other				
2. Clothing (estimate for entire family)				
3. Food				
4. Insurance				
a. Homeowner's				
b. Life				
c. Health				
d. Other				
5. Home expenses				
a. Rent				
b. Mortgage				
c. Repairs				
d. Real estate taxes				
e. Escrow payments				
f. Heat				
g. Other				
6. Medical				
a. Out of pocket				

YEARLY AND MONTHLY EXPENSES	YEARLY EXPENSE	MONTHLY EXPENSE	% OF TOTAL EXPENSE	F,V,O,C
b. Dental				
c. Medication				
d. Other supplies				
e. Health club				
7. Charitable contributions				
a.				
b.				
8. Taxes				
a. Income				
b. Local				
c. State				
d. Social Security				
e. Personal property				
f. Other				
9. Utilities				
a. Cell phones				
b. Land phone lines				
c. Internet				
d. Electric				
e. Cable TV				
f. Water & Sewer				
10. Basic family				
a. Entertainment				
b. Vacation				
c. Gifts				
d. Support for parent(s)				

YEARLY AND MONTHLY EXPENSES	YEARLY EXPENSE	MONTHLY EXPENSE	% OF TOTAL EXPENSE	F,V,O,C
e. Other				
11. Computer				
a. Hardware				
b. Software				
c. Repairs				
12. Financial				
a. Capital additions to portfolio				
b. Safe deposit box				
c. Publications and subscriptions				
d. Advisors and planners				
e. Other				
13. Misc.				
a.				
b.				
c.				
d.				
TOTAL EXPENSES				

Your worksheets show your money flow in and out of your household. Now you need to add the dynamics of how to use this information in the coming year. Date your worksheet and you will use it as a starting point for the Ham-and-Egg Budget we will construct to give us a picture of coming year. It may take you five to ten hours or so to complete your first set of worksheets. But once you set up your record-keeping system and keep up with monthly Quicken data input from your checking account, filling in the succeeding year's worksheet will be much easier since you will be familiar with the process and the data will be readily at hand.

On the expense side, divide items into four categories so that you can readily see how to reallocate income to save money or be more effective in how it is spent. For example, if each of your children has his or her own cell phone account and Internet account, it will come to your attention on the worksheet and you may decide to bundle them all into a family plan. Also, any item that is a high percentage of total family expenses deserves special scrutiny to see if it is warranted. In order to decide what you actually have available that can be changed or reworked, place an "**F**", "**V**", "**O**", or "**C**" after the expense, as explained below :

1. *Fixed (F):* These expenses reoccur in a regular amount each month and include items such as mortgage, rent, and insurance.
2. *Variable (V):* Monthly expenses vary according to lifestyle choices: entertainment, cell phones, and food, for example.
3. *Occasional (O):* Such onetime expenses may or may not repeat again in the year: new dishwasher, initial health club fee, prom dress, etc. Lump them into a "miscellaneous" category.
4. *Capital additions (C):* Capital additions to investments are expenses because they are a call on a significant part of

your earned income and part of our PLAN. Since their availability is in the future, they are an outflow to a yearly budget but an addition to your family's investment portfolio. (Remember, your PLAN should envision capital additions of 20–50 percent each year to build your investment portfolio.)

Step back and look at these charts and you will see a clear picture of how your family's financial life works. Most high "F" percentage expenses and all "V" expenses and "C" expenses are important to revisit. Look at allocations to these categories of Income and Expense for the next year in your Ham-and-Egg Budget and compare them to the last year's data. Change what you need to so you have items fall within the limits you want.

Now it's time to move the information from your worksheet into a personalized Ham-and-Egg Budget. The income part of the budget in *Chart 5.3* will *exclude all investment income* (Sections 1, 2, and 4) from *Chart 5.1* but include income you are lucky enough to receive yearly from a family trust (Section 3d) set up for your benefit. We will consider that part of earned income.

– CHART 5.3
HAM-AND-EGG BUDGET(1)
(For the year ending /   /   )

INCOME	YEARLY TOTAL
1. Fixed income	
a. Earned income	
• Salary 1	
• Salary 2	
b. Alimony	
c. Child support	
d. Annuity	
e. Other	
2. Variable income	
a. Trust	
b. Other	
3. Occasional income	
a. Bonus	
b. Part-time work	
c. Other	
TOTAL SPENDABLE INCOME	

EXPENSES	YEARLY TOTAL
1. Fixed expenses	
a. Mortgage/rent	
b. Life insurance	
c. Medical	
d. Loan payments	
e. Other	
2. Variable expenses	
a. Automobile	
b. Clothing	
c. Food	
d. Medical/dental	
e. Utilities	
f. Entertainment	
g. Vacation	
h. Other	
3. Occasional expenses	
a. Computer hardware/software	
b. Charitable	
c. Other	
4. Capital additions	
a. Fixed savings percentage (20–50%)	
• 401(k)	
• Other tax-advantage plan contributions	
• Retirement savings	
b. Other	
TOTAL EXPENSES	
EXCESS OF INCOME OVER EXPENSES	

(1) Clearly both items included and amounts will be different as each reader personalizes their information.

Note that the Ham-and-Egg Budget is shorter than the worksheet form. That is because the budget does not include investment income that you leave untouched to allow the miracle of compounding to work. In addition, you have grouped items and perhaps changed, by reduction or increase, certain expense categories that are variable or occasional. Of course, you cannot change those that are fixed. But now you have a baseline of how the next year should shape up without an unexpected event forcing changes.

So let's recap:

- Once you have loaded a year's worth of data into Quicken, the program will help you create your Ham-and-Egg Budget.
- Quicken will allow you to see expenses and track your progress each month of the year.
- The process of collecting like bills together to reach a total for our **PLAN** is instructive.
- Individual expense items are likely to stick in your mind and suggest points to consider.

You will probably understand the details better and put more thought into your spending habits after this grunt work. The Quicken program is also great for displaying data graphically in pie charts, color charts, lists, or most any way you desire. But Quicken is still limited to an output based on the quality of the data you input.

THE WHIPPED-CREAM-AND-CHERRY BUDGET

Now is the time to bring together much of the thinking in previous chapters and use it to create a Whipped-Cream-and-Cherry

Budget. This is a goal-line budget and a sort of a wish list. As your savings and investments prosper, you will cross the goal line on major financial events that will happen in the future. The income items will be increased by your investment yields, which were on your worksheet in *Chart 5.1* but not included in your Ham-and-Egg Budget. While your family can survive in any given year on the Ham-and-Egg Budget, you want to provide for certain future expenses that are toppings on the sundae of basic day-to-day living.

You may need to calculate a future value (as we did when you budgeted for your children's college costs earlier in this chapter) for each expense that is more than five years away. For periods under five years, there is not enough compounding to necessitate this calculation—just divide your best estimate of the expense by the years to the goal and enter equal installments in the budget.

The Whipped-Cream-and-Cherry Budget is unusual for three reasons:

1. Items will come into the budget when they become a goal and leave the budget as soon as they are fully funded.
2. This budget is a single-year snapshot that is not a perfect direct comparison to any other year because some line items may change.
3. You will use your Whipped-Cream-and-Cherry budget to help construct your Net Worth Statement, which is the subject of the next chapter. (A fully funded goal is an asset and is no longer part of the cash flow in a budget.)

The Whipped-Cream-and-Cherry Budget is the next step up from the Ham-and-Egg Budget because investment earnings are included in the income listing and your individual wish-list items have been identified. Most of the data is just copied from the worksheets. The funding sources for your wish list are both the yearly capital additions, plus any net yearly excess income over expenses. You are showing on paper what you want to do in the future and how you will allocate funding to these major goal-line items.

In Chapter 6, we address this question in depth, but as a preview here I'll note that most financial planners will counsel that the world is too complex, things just cost more, Americans are not used to saving, and a host of other excuses. These are convenient but beg the fact that if you just assume your spendable income is reduced and live within the means of the balance, it is quite easy to adapt to this notion. Can't do it all? Come as close as you can. And once the miracle of compounding sets in on those savings, you and your family will be quite pleased with your net worth and financial security.

It is not necessary to have a physically separate brokerage account, bond ladders, or money-market accounts for each future item in the Whipped-Cream-and Cherry Budget. Some people like to see the growth of investments and want this structure. It does create a lot of monthly paperwork, but Quicken can accommodate an almost unlimited number of accounts. For instance, I did have separate college accounts for my children in which I placed zero-coupon bonds. These accounts were in my kids' names to save some taxes. My family also kept investments solely in both my wife's and my name in case of an emergency where one partner needed access to immediate resources.

So let's look at the structure of this second kind of budget and work with it for a while. Categories in a sample Whipped-Cream-and-Cherry Budget may look something like *Chart 5.4*:

– CHART 5.4 –
WHIPPED-CREAM-AND-CHERRY BUDGET
(For the year ending   /   /   )

INCOME

INCOME	YEARLY TOTAL
1. Fixed income	
a. Earned income	
• Salary 1	
• Salary 2	
b. Alimony	
c. Child support	
d. Bond income	
• Corporate	
• Municipal	
• Zero-coupon accretion	
e. Annuity	
f. Rental income	
g. Other	
2. Variable income	
a. Investment income	
• Stocks	
• Money market	
• Mutual fund distributions	
• REIT distributions	
• Savings accounts	
• Partnership income	
• Other	
b. Other real-estate income	

INCOME	YEARLY TOTAL
c. Trust income	
d. Other	
3. Occasional income	
a. Bonus	
b. Part-time work	
c. Other	
TOTAL SPENDABLE INCOME	

EXPENSES

EXPENSES	YEARLY TOTAL
1. Fixed expenses	
a. Mortgage/rent (why doesn't this begin with "a"?)	
b. Life insurance	
c. Medical	
d. Loan payments	
e. Other	
2. Variable expenses	
a. Automobile (why not begin with "a"?)	
b. Clothing	
c. Food	
d. Medical/dental	
e. Utilities	
f. Entertainment	
g. Vacation	
h. Other	
3. Occasional expenses	
a. Computer hardware/software (why not begin with "a"?)	

EXPENSES	YEARLY TOTAL
b. Charitable	
c. Other	
4. Capital additions	
a. Fixed savings percentage (20–50%)	
b. 401(k)	
c. Other tax-advantage plan contributions	
d. Retirement savings	
e. Other	
TOTAL EXPENSES	
EXCESS OF INCOME OVER EXPENSES	
APPLICATION OF CAPITAL ADDITIONS PLUS EXCESS INCOME TO FUTURE GOALS	

FUTURE GOALS

ITEM	YEARLY $ NEEDED	TOTAL $ TO GOAL	YEARS TO GOAL
New home down payment *			
Child 1 college fund *			
Child 2 college fund *			
Wedding expenses *			
Swimming pool *			
New kitchen *			
GOAL			
GOAL			

*Arbitrary placeholder examples that will change depending on your particular future needs.

Note that when the *"Years to Goal"* number is zero and the *"Total $ to Goal"* is fulfilled, that goal-line item will disappear from the Whipped-Cream-and-Cherry Budget and appear only on your Net Worth Statement. There is no need to make a yearly budget provision for a fully funded future goal. However, the money is an asset. So if you have saved enough to send your daughter to college a few years before she will attend, that item will not appear in your budgets although your Net Worth Statement will include an account that shows this item as an asset. Or, if you have saved a full down payment for a vacation home but have not located a property yet, there will only be a funded asset account on the Net Worth Statement to recognize this funded goal.

It is your responsibility to set the number of goals and cost of each goal-line item on your wish list, as well as an associated time frame to achieve it. Your anticipation of the future should contain some big-ticket items that you would like for your family. No one can really do it for you because every expenditure, want, desire, and family situation is unique. Spend some really intense hours consulting with your spouse about your aspirations. What is really important to you and those you love? Be realistic. Plans will change, but this is today and the best we can do is plan with what we know now. Here is a partial list of some of the most common goal-line items in a financial road map:

1. BUYING A FIRST HOME

If you don't own a home, consider the price range you can afford and then the time frame in which you want to buy it. Then calculate the down payment you will need. As I discuss in the real estate section of Chapter 7, ordinarily you should not buy a house with less than a 25 percent down payment. That equity is your protection against market swings.

Once again, you will need to calculate a future value for the likely price of a home at the time you hope to purchase. For example:

- In seven years you intend to buy a home that today sells for $250,000.
- Assume a 2 percent-per-year price appreciation. Use a future value calculator from Google to determine that the house will probably cost $287,000 in seven years.
- Following the 25 percent guideline, you will need a down payment of approximately $72,000 (0.25 x $287,000 = $71,750).
- You will have to save approximately $10,000 per year for seven years to reach your goal.

Had you used today's price of $250,000 for your calculation, a 25 percent down payment would be $62,500 and you might have saved only $8,900 per year—insufficient as a 25 percent down payment seven years hence. This is why the present and future value calculations are very useful to more accurately gauge goal-line expenditures at a future point in time. In money matters, we want to be as realistic and accurate as possible.

There is some flexibility on how much of your income you should allocate for a down payment on a first home, but mortgage and all other home expenses should not exceed 45 percent of your gross income. A mortgage loan officer at a bank might want to see a much lower number.

2. TRADING UP TO A BETTER HOME

If you already own a home but want to trade up, you should decide on a price range that makes sense for your income and the rules in the "Home Sweet Home" chapter. Decide on a time frame in which to trade up. The additional down payment is a financial goal that will be listed in the "Excess of Income over Expenses" part of the Whipped-Cream-and-Cherry Budget (*Chart 5.4*).

Let's look at an example. Your family is running out of space in your $250,000 home, or perhaps you want to move to a particular school district where homes are more expensive. For this example we shall use rounded numbers and not include various transaction costs such as brokerage commissions, taxes, moving expenses, or recording fees.

- The equity you have in your home has grown from the $62,500 you used as a down payment (25 percent x $250,000 = $62,500). You are now up to $87,500 in equity because the property can currently be sold for $275,000.
- The homes in that new area are more expensive, in the $400,000 range, so you will need $12,500 more for a down payment (25 percent x $400,000 = $100,000).
- Your income has grown a bit so you could borrow, but as a practitioner of our safe and secure **PLAN** you realize that debt is rarely good. Although you will have to borrow more money, you do plan to pay down the additional $12,500 that should have been in the down payment.
- You would like to repay this amount in three years. Since it is under five years, simply divide by three and add a line item of "New house down-payment deficit" to your Whipped-Cream-and-Cherry Budget for each of the next three years. You will repay $4,200 each year.

3. FIXING UP OR REMODELING A HOME

Decide on a priority order for the major changes you want to do to your home. A contractor's estimate will give you a fairly accurate basis for calculating these amounts in the current market. Next, decide on a reasonable time frame for accomplishing each item. Some items, such as a pool, may be ten years off and need a future-value calculation to budget correctly. Other items like new bathroom fixtures may only be one to two years off and can be divided into one- or two-installment budget entries.

4. WEDDINGS AND OTHER MAJOR FUNCTIONS

Some large functions can cost from $10,000 to $75,000 or even more. The dates for these celebrations are predictable and often exact points in time. You can calculate a Bar Mitzvah or Confirmation party from your children's age, or a twenty-fifthth wedding anniversary affair from today's date. If you expect a major expense, do a future-value calculation from a current estimate and add a new line item to your Whipped-Cream-and-Cherry Budget.

5. A LONG SABBATICAL

It has always been your dream to take a year off. Start saving and preparing now. It won't happen if you don't have the ability to fund it.

6. EXTENSIVE FOREIGN TRAVEL

If you want to see a special part of the world on an extended basis, you need to decide on the style of travel, time frame, duration, and cost. Include the amount in your budget.

7. CAPITAL TO START YOUR OWN BUSINESS

If you have always wanted to be your own boss, then start saving for that purpose. This is likely to be a major expenditure, which may include loss of salaried income once you begin devoting time to the new enterprise.

8. STARTING A FAMILY CHARITY

If you have been particularly successful, you may want to establish a charity of your own. You can set up a charity to fund a cause or launch a trust to help future family members long after your death.

The Whipped-Cream-and-Cherry Budget reflects your current hopes and dreams. If you plan for goal-line items, they are much more likely to come to fruition. Funding the future is always a combination of wise investment and the addition of excess income over the baseline expenses you must meet in a Ham-and-Egg Budget. Your aspirations are worth providing for. As our old friend Woody Allen said, "85 percent of life is just showing up." The other 15 percent is planning and preparation.

NET WORTH = PERSONAL BALANCE SHEET

A *balance sheet* for a company is a quantitative summary of its financial condition at a specific point in time. It includes a complete listing of all assets and liabilities. Liabilities are subtracted from assets to arrive at a net value for the firm. This accounting value may not have any resemblance to the company's stock market value, which is often many times higher (although sometimes lower). A balance sheet exercise provides a valuable snapshot as it is the basis for creditworthiness and the underlying strength of the company's asset management. We will apply this concept of financial reliability to your family portfolio.

In our **PLAN** we will call your personal balance sheet the *Net Worth Statement*. This is the fourth and last of the reports you should prepare each year. Think of your Net Worth Statement as a report card on how well you have managed your financial life. Quicken will do much of the tabulation for you and display your net worth once you have properly input the data. In the alternative, use an Internet net worth calculator such as the one at www.themoneyplanbook.com or go to Google and enter "networth statement calculator." Inputting, of course, is the sticky point because "garbage in means garbage out." (That is why we began with the notion of maintaining an organized record-keeping system.)

The Net Worth Statement for an individual is as simple in concept as a balance sheet is for a corporation. It displays all known assets and liabilities and then subtracts the liabilities from the assets. Said another way, it is a calculation of what you have left over if everything you own is converted into cash and all liabilities paid off in full. Of course, if you are leading a normal life, you will never sell everything to become 100 percent liquid. So every asset has to be fairly valued and every liability fairly determined. Since no one but you and your spouse will probably see this tabulation, don't fool yourself by sweeping liability under the rug or exaggerating market value of an asset such as your home or an antique. Each year you will want to judge your net worth as a benchmark on progress for growing your family wealth using our **PLAN**.

The somewhat tricky part is determining the value of each asset without actually selling it. For a home, ask a realtor for an appraisal and look online and in a newspaper for similar properties in your area. Financial assets will be valued by the market in which they trade and appear on your brokerage statements. (In many cases these values can be downloaded into Quicken.)

Most difficult are the antiques, paintings, jewelry, private-placement investments (stocks or bonds in smaller, nonpublic companies) that have not matured and have no public market value, and other assets that have no arm's-length (free and independent professional) market value determination. Do the best you can with such items—but if you can't visualize someone actually paying the amount you entered on your Net Worth Statement, be very conservative. Inflating the value of assets will not give you an accurate picture. Aunt Jean's collection of old cookie jars may cost one price in an antique store, but you don't own the store to sell them. Besides, cookie jars are highly illiquid as not everyone wants three Daffy Duck and two Goofy cookie jars. Ask yourself, "Will I really be able to locate buyers?"

Your *Personal Net Worth Statement* might include:

Assets

1. *Home(s):* Current value of each property.
2. *Other real estate:* The market value of any other real estate you own. Include undeveloped land, rental property, and commercial buildings.
3. *Home mortgage principal repaid.*
4. *Other loan principal repaid.*
5. Total amount you have currently paid down on any borrowings.
6. *Automobiles:* Don't include leased vehicles as *you don't own* them.
7. *Jewelry:* The value of any jewelry, gems, or precious metals such as gold. If you have owned these items for a number of years, they may have appreciated in value.
8. *Household items:* The value of your household goods and items. This is an estimate, so be conservative.

9. *Brokerage accounts*: Enter the account value from the brokerage statement.

10. *Mutual fund accounts*: Use the end-of-year statement.

11. *Retirement accounts*: The total balance of your retirement accounts as shown on their statements. Include IRAs, 401(k), and any other tax-advantaged retirement savings.

12. *Bonds*: Include treasury, municipal, and commercial bonds.

13. *Cash value of life insurance*: Some life insurance has a cash value.

14. *Trusts*: Your parents set one up for you? Lucky you!

15. *Savings bonds*: Include any U.S. Savings Bonds you own.

16. *Checking and savings*: The current balances of your checking and savings accounts.

17. *Cash*: Any other cash investments such as a money market.

18. *Certificates of deposit*: Enter the total value from the statement.

19. *Other*: Enter the total of any other assets.

Liabilities

1. *Mortgages owed*: Enter the amount from your mortgage statement.

2. *Student loans*: Total amount that you currently owe in college or student loans. Enter the total outstanding even if the loan is currently in deferment.

3. *Credit card debt*: Enter your total credit card debt.

4. *Other loans*: Enter the total amounts of any other loans.

Your *Personal Net Worth Statement* might look like the chart below:

– CHART 5.5 –
NET WORTH STATEMENT
As of (/   /   )

ASSETS	
Cash	
Checking	
Savings	
Securities	
Trusts	
Real estate	
Household goods	
Vehicles	
Cash value life insurance	
401(k) or other tax-advantaged plans	
Individual Retirement Accounts	
Other assets	
TOTAL ASSETS	

LIABILITIES	
Notes payable	
Accounts and bills due	
Credit cards payable	
Vehicle loans	
Unpaid taxes	
Real-estate mortgages payable	

LIABILITIES	
Life insurance loans	
Other liabilities	
TOTAL LIABILITIES	

ASSETS MINUS LIABILITIES	
TOTAL NET WORTH	

Once you have completed this exercise, you will know how much you own in your total portfolio as of the date of your Personal Net Worth Statement. It is prudent to do this at least once each year when you prepare your Ham-and-Egg and Whipped-Cream-and-Cherry Budgets. Once you prepare your Personal Net Worth Statement in Quicken and keep the information current, you can update it as many times as you wish as it then becomes a simple mathematical calculation.

LIQUID ASSETS ARE NOT DRINKABLE

Liquidity touches all three elements of our three-legged-stool approach. First, *safe and secure* means you don't lose your money and it is available to you when needed. Second, *consistent available cash flow* is the very definition of liquidity and it assures you can meet your obligations. Third, *careful and educated investment execution* is keeping a proper balance among all types of investments.

Financial management is the art of balancing your liquid and illiquid assets to create the best earning power on your money, and also *meeting your present needs for spendable cash*. *Liquidity* refers to how close an asset is to being cash. Paper bills (cash) are the ultimate kind of liquidity since they are accepted everywhere in exchange for goods and services. So cash is ground zero of the liquidity spectrum. Real estate is considered largely illiquid because of the time it takes to find a buyer, draw up papers, have the buyer secure financing, and finally close on the transfer of ownership and receive your money in cash. It is not unusual for this process to take two to six months or more. During that period of time, you do not have access to the purchaser's funds. In addition, there is always the possibility that the transaction will fall apart, and you are back to square one until you find a new buyer.

You should understand the concept of investment liquidity and manage your money and assets to have the proper amount of cash and near cash (stocks, CDs, money markets, savings accounts, etc) readily available. How much is the proper amount? When we construct budgets in this book, you will have to make a judgment call on what seems right for your family. With kids in college and yearly tuition, you may need a greater amount of ready liquidity. Kids sometimes need an emergency injection of cash from parents. If you are caring for a sick parent whose resources are limited, having more cash around may come in handy.

But if you are at a different point in life with little or no borrowed money (mortgages, business loans, car loans, etc.), kids are on their own, and you are in good health, perhaps you can have less liquidity than if you have many obligations. I like to keep 2–5 percent of my assets immediately liquid at all times. In periods of turmoil in the economy, that number can rise to 10–15 percent of assets. There is no hard and fast rule. It's whatever is prudent and lets you sleep at night. So if my net worth is growing nicely, my income covers all foreseeable expenses, and my wife is not planning on a major home improvement, I am closer to the 2 percent number.

A mixture of assets with various kinds of liquidity is a key element of our financial PLAN for safe and secure. If you have a lot of passbook savings or a money market fund and receive a demand for payment on an expense, it is a simple matter to meet the obligation. However, if all of your money is committed elsewhere for an extended time period, you may have a problem.

Here are the basic degrees of liquidity from highest to lowest for some common assets:

– CHART 5.6 –
LIQUIDITY SCALE
HIGHEST TO LOWEST

1. Cash in checking or a money market fund
2. Stocks that are actively traded
3. ETFs (Exchange Traded Funds), SPDRs (Standard and Poor's Depository Receipts), etc., which I discuss in Chapter 7
4. Mutual funds
5. Bonds
6. CDs (individual banks have their own rules on withdrawals)
7. Cash value in insurance policies
8. Automobiles
9. Specialty investments such as hedge funds, venture funds, etc.
10. Jewelry and ordinary antiques
11. Physical gold or silver (and most commodities)
12. Real estate
13. Limited partnerships and hedge funds
14. High-priced art and antiques
15. Privately owned business

As an asset becomes more illiquid, it becomes increasingly difficult to turn it back into the cash used to purchase it. Our PLAN envisions that you keep in reserve an appropriate level of liquidity to meet most situations that might arise each time you purchase more illiquid assets. In other words, if you are buying a piece of real estate, which is highly illiquid, be certain you have enough highly liquid assets to meet most any eventuality. A starting point is to have approximately 20 percent of total assets fall in the most liquid categories: invested in cash (savings, money market, or checking accounts), stocks of publicly traded companies, ETFs, and bonds. It is a sliding scale and the 20 percent target will move, especially once you take age into account. Later in this book are some rough guidelines for asset allocation by age.

When you are young and just starting out, the purchase of a first home may skew your assets toward illiquidity because most of your savings will be used as a down payment. That is not necessarily bad as long as you recognize that you must make every effort to recover the liquidity lost to this unusual purchase event. On the other end of the scale, as you get past middle age the percentage of liquidity may dramatically increase. Retirees may have 50 percent or more of their assets in highly liquid categories. There can be many reasons for such a weighting including ease of access to the funds, desire to gift money, and the simplification of paying estate taxes.

In general, the more liquid an asset, the lower the expected rate of return. Less liquid assets tend to have greater rate-of-return associated with their greater risk profiles—meaning you can make more but you run a greater risk of losing your principal. Percentage profit/rate-of-return is lower for liquid investments because money that is quick and easy to access has little risk associated with it. You can get it back the next day or close to it.

Money in a money market fund may earn 1 percent (at current rates) per year, while funds tied up in a five-year CD might earn 3¾ percent per year because you are agreeing to leave them in someone else's hands (the bank's) for five years. However, assuming the bank is FDIC insured, that money is not at risk. You can reasonably expect to be paid when the CD reaches maturity. Funds committed to a ten-year investment in a venture fund might be expected to earn 15 percent per year if everything works out all right in the fund's portfolio. In this investment you have a combination of the ten years of time your money is in another's control plus the riskiness of the character profile of venture investment.

It you have lots of assets but they are all very illiquid, you are really cash poor at that moment because you have nothing in your immediate control to spend. Many older folks live in a fully paid house worth a large amount of money but have few other liquid assets to generate income for their day-to-day living expenses. This is an uncomfortable, "house-poor" lifestyle. A house can be sold and the proceeds invested to produce income if a senior would be more appropriate renting rather than owning.

It is important for you to determine the balance that is proper for your age and responsibilities as you move between the items listed in our *Liquidity Scale* above. Being "house-poor" is very similar to the opposite extreme of living heavily in debt with little discretionary income to spend on day-to-day living. Being completely in cash produces a very low income level from your assets. They are both circumstances to be avoided.

BUDGETING FOR BEING
OFF YOUR ROCKER

"Death should not be seen as the end, but as a very effective way to cut down on expenses."
–WOODY ALLEN

There are many dozens of books and thousands of articles on retirement and how to prepare for it. They all boil down to making early investment decisions in assets that will produce a comfortable cash flow for the many years you are likely to live beyond your working life. Our entire **PLAN** for wealth creation is really a recognition that, after a certain number of years of exertion, it is time to get on with a different stage in life. Young people do not imagine that they will ever grow old and wish to make a complete change in lifestyle. Most thrive under the pressure and excitement of step-by-step advancement. However, the addition of candles on your birthday cake brings the realization that saving and investing wisely was a good thing. As Mark Twain said, "Age is an issue of mind over matter. If you don't mind, it doesn't matter."

And you won't mind if you have no financial worries and can travel, spend, and help your children and grandchildren without depriving yourself of comfort. Wealth also allows you to focus on unexpected family events such as illness without facing a financial crisis as well. Many of the concepts we have explored in the previous chapters come into play in making retirement the great time it should be. So let's list what we need to do to prepare intelligently for retirement:

1. Start early.
2. Save 20–50 percent or more of income in some form.
3. Allow the miracle of compounding to work.
4. Keep your focus on your goals.
5. Calculate future values.
6. Don't fund only the most pressing goals (college, home, etc.) and ignore retirement.
7. Reduce debt as you get older.
8. Concentrate more on cash flow as you get older.
9. Make full use of tax-advantage investments like 401(k)s, traditional IRAs, and Roth IRAs.
10. Don't ignore inflation.

11. Plan your health care carefully.
12. Count on living a long time.
13. Review your plan each and every year.
14. Stick with safe and secure.
15. Remember that your children love you but can't support you.
16. Don't count on the government. (Heck, they're counting on YOU!)

I knew a very successful man who owned several large and highly profitable companies. Although he was ninety-two, he was still very sharp and ran the companies as CEO very effectively. One day when the Board members were gathered for a meeting, one said, "Harry, you know we ought to start thinking about how to run things when you're not here." Without missing a beat, Harry replied, "You know that if I'm not here you can always reach me at home." Preparation for the future is smart. Planning financial matters for retirement and eventual death is not everybody's cup of tea ... but it is an important part of safe and secure.

We have taken major steps toward retirement planning with our yearly exercise of drafting Ham-and-Egg and Whipped-Cream-and-Cherry Budgets as well as preparing a Personal Net Worth Statement. But to complete the process, we still have to perform a series of calculations based on the best available information. For most people reading this book, retirement is a long way off—fifteen to twenty-five years or more. The growth in your need for future income, at even a modest inflation rate, will surprise you. The following worksheet in *Chart 5.7* should help give you a picture of the future. It's not a lot of work since most of the data can be copied off of your budgets.

– CHART 5.7 –
RETIREMENT PLANNING WORKSHEET[1]

(as of   /   /   )

Estimated *years* until retirement	
Estimated annual *current living expense*[1]	
Average *inflation* factor[2]	
Future value of *living expense*	
Portfolio *value* at present time	
Portfolio *income* (rate of return)	
Future *value of portfolio* at today's rate of return	
Estimated *portfolio income* today	
Estimated portfolio *income at retirement*	
Retirement reductions in living expenses[3]	
Other retirement *income4*	
Potential *excess (or deficit) of income*	

[1] From your budgets.
[2] Estimated from the last decade's actual inflation number.
[3] Paid-off mortgage, no more college expenses, reduction in number of homes, etc.
[4] Trust income, pensions, Social Security, etc.

You can't simply calculate the starting-age year at which you will retire and call retirement planning quits. That is only the starting point. If you are going to survive another twenty years, the inflation factor will significantly affect the longest future-value calculations. Say you are thirty-four and you plan to retire at age sixty-five. If current income is $100,000 per year and inflation remains at a constant 3 percent, in just your first year of retirement you will need approximately $250,000 to have the same purchasing power you have at the present (use an Internet future value calculator to arrive at this number). The income increase from $100,000 to $250,000 is after a period of thirty-one years (65 − 34 = 31) in which purchasing power is eroded by 3 percent inflation.

However, if you survive to eighty-five years of age, a period of fifty-one years, you will need approximately $450,000 of income in your eighty-fifth year to maintain the same purchasing power as $100,000 at age thirty-four if inflation remains at a constant 3 percent. (Recall our Babe Ruth sidebar earlier.) Of course this huge income need is offset by the compounding of earnings during the intervening years in your portfolio. So if your portfolio grew at 3 percent or more, you will still find yourself in good shape. And along the way there will likely be reductions in the inflation rate (and also some increases). In 2009, the inflation rate was less than 1 percent. It can often rise unexpectedly. This example shows how insidious inflation can be if it is not taken into account in long-term planning.

As part of your **PLAN** for retirement, use your current income as a base number and do a future value calculation for each five-year period until age ninety-five or so. This will give you some goal posts for income needed to maintain your purchasing power. These calculations will not be exact because, in reality, the inflation rate will fluctuate and your needs will also change. If you are in a peak spending year, such as when two or more children are in college, that level of outflow will not be sustained in retirement. However, these goal posts will give you a direction for the increase in cash flow that will meet your retirement needs at five-year intervals.

This exercise will prepare you to meet inflation head-on as it erodes your purchasing power. Part of inflation will be offset by directing investments away from capital appreciation and into income-producing assets as you grow older and face the end of wage income. Another factor will be your reduction in actual living expenses as your children become independent and self-sustaining.

One other point is relevant: at a certain age it is acceptable to spend part of the principal of your assets for living expenses and reduce the size of your estate to your heirs. One would hope that you don't need to spend any portion of these funds because our **PLAN** has increased your wealth to the level that it generates sufficient income to meet all your needs. But circumstances beyond your control can affect the best of such long-term planning, creating a need to use some part of your portfolio savings for current expenses. Monitor the withdrawals closely. As long as the depletion is very unlikely to run you out of capital and make you a burden on other family members, use and enjoy the fruits of your own efforts for your own well-being. Don't skimp on yourself just to pass on money.

Planning for retirement does not seem to be at the top of the agenda for most Americans. Our PLAN is to assure that you are not in that group. According to the Employee Benefit Research Institute (www.ebri.org), some 30 percent of workers age fifty-five and older who responded to a survey find themselves with total savings and investments of less than $10,000—and a whopping 74 percent have less than $250,000 in total retirement savings.

− CHART 5.8 −
REPORTED TOTAL SAVINGS AND INVESTMENTS AMONG WORKERS PROVIDING A RESPONSE, 2009
(not including value of primary residence or defined benefit plans)

	ALL WORKERS	AGES 25-34	AGES 35-44	AGES 45-54	AGES 55+
Less than $10,000	40%	53%	37%	36%	30%
$10,000-$24,999	13	20	16	7	6
$25,000-$49,999	11	12	8	11	13
$50,000-$99,999	12	9	14	14	10
$100,000-$249,999	12	5	16	15	15
$250,000 or more	12	2	9	17	26

Source: Employee Benefit Research Institute, Mathew Greenwald & Associates, Inc., 2009 Retirement Confidence Survey.

For those who have not adequately provided for their own future, retirement will not be the "golden years." That is why our PLAN is to have you start saving at a robust level when you are young; stay conservative but not too conventional early in your career; and avoid choosing precarious investments at a later stage, when you should not shoulder so much risk. You are striving for safe and secure all along the way. If your financial life were baseball, you would be looking for a series of singles and doubles and not a home run each time you were up at bat. With yearly planning the goal is to travel the bases to home plate and enjoy a stress-free retirement with a nice estate for your progeny to build upon.

One income-producing investment besides bonds or high dividend stocks is a type of mutual fund that is structured to automatically send you regular checks every month starting at the time you retire. When you die, you pass on whatever assets remain to your heirs. These *managed payout funds* are offered by Fidelity Investments, Charles Schwab & Co., Vanguard, and several other firms. The problem with these investments is that your entire nest egg could be depleted by a specific date, and you might live longer than you think.

I favor a municipal bond ladder as a primary income strategy, although a portion of your overall portfolio can be committed to managed payout funds, mutual funds, individual stocks, or exchange-traded funds if they appeal to you. They all may have a place as a secondary portion of your portfolio, up to the range of 10–20 percent of assets. You may elect to have none, if your risk-tolerance level is very low. In any event, the expense fees in managed pay mutual funds are around 1 percent, much better than the 2–5 percent charged by annuities (which I do not recommend). The plus side is that your monthly payments can grow, depending on investment performance. By taking payouts from this type of mutual fund early in retirement, you can leave your tax-deferred investment accounts intact to continue to reinvest and grow.

Three types of tax-advantaged accounts you will likely encounter are the **401(k), the Roth 401(k), and the IRA.**

- Most employers sponsor a *401(k) plan,* which is a *defined contribution plan.* The defined contribution plan designates a fixed percentage of *pretax* earnings you may contribute and invest in a selected list of mutual funds. In a 401(k) the employee has to undertake the responsibility for retirement savings and its management. Keep in mind a fixed benefit contribution is not a guarantee your choice of funds will perform well.

  In most cases, the employer matches some portion of the employee-designated contribution (from 1–6 percent), taken from the paycheck before taxes are calculated. From the employee's point of view, this match is a very significant return on investment. If you contribute 3 percent and your employer matches the 3 percent, you have immediately doubled your investment, and the entire amount will grow tax free until you withdraw the money. The miracle of compounding does its magic!

  There are a couple of negatives to 401(k) plans. It is difficult to access your money without paying a significant penalty of 10 percent prior to age 59 ½ (except in certain specific circumstances). So your contribution is locked in. Another negative is you must begin to withdraw "minimum distributions" after age 70½, which will be taxable income and stop your compounding investment.

- One variation on the common 401(k) defined-contribution plan is the *Roth 401(k),* which allows *after-tax* dollars to be placed in it. Although you don't get the up-front tax deduction, the earnings accumulate tax free until withdrawal. (Remember the miracle of compounding.) The Roth 401(k) permits tax-free and penalty-free withdrawals of your contributions anytime and, after five years, withdrawal of your earnings. The catch is that, when you withdraw, you need to be in the same tax bracket you were in at the time of your initial after-tax contribution. If you retire to a much lower tax bracket, then you have lost some money.

Of course, the reverse is also true and in that case you come out ahead. For a young person, a Roth 401(k) may find you at a lower tax bracket early in your career. Later, withdrawing in peak earning years, none of the Roth 401(k) distributions would be taxed. That can produce a handsome return.

Unlike a regular 401(k), you may continue to contribute to a Roth 401(k) after age 70½ and thus keep building up earnings tax free.

■ If your employer changes and your plan account is distributed when you leave, you may choose to roll the distribution into an *Individual Retirement Account (IRA)*. This can be a self-directed vehicle and you may select from a wide range of investment choices. It is in effect a separate portfolio in which the investments accumulate profit and income streams tax free until you withdraw the money. Most any brokerage firm or mutual fund company can help you set up and manage a self-directed IRA with a minimal fee structure.

There is a wealth of information available on the Internet about 401(k), Roth 401(k), and IRA plans, and any competent financial advisor should be able to help. These tax-advantaged investment vehicles should definitely be a part of your overall retirement arrangement. It should come as no surprise that the government has imposed a plethora of technical rules on these plans and the movement of invested funds. Should you change employers or need emergency access to your money, you must carefully follow the rules or face a penalty (currently 10 percent) or loss of tax-advantage status.

Although the programs change radically every few years, Social Security and Medicare do provide some minimal level of retirement help. Of course, they will not return more than a small fraction of what a successful individual has paid into them. But since your contributions are mandatory, you should know the benefits to which you are entitled. You should receive a yearly contribution statement from Social Security. Everyone should apply for Medicare three months before his or her sixty-fifth birthday even if your intention is to continue working. We consider Social Security and Medicare as "other retirement income" on our worksheet. These government programs are only a subsistence-level crumb and will provide for a minor part of your needs. You, not the government, are responsible for the quality of your retirement, based on your careful savings and management of your portfolio.

EXAMPLES THAT PUT IT ALL TOGETHER

Let's take a look at how the **PLAN** might actually work. In order to simplify our calculations, the dollar amounts are rounded, categories for income and expenses are kept to a minimum, and I haven't calculated present or future value for every possible event. In most cases you, too, can round some numbers so as not to make the calculations too tedious. In some categories you will have to estimate because events or facts may not be in your complete control.

Our **PLAN** recognizes that life is occasionally messy, and it can deal with that fact. Outcomes of many events are un-certain. People sometimes make irrational financial decisions they regret. And there are special circumstances unique to each family. We are applying the broad principles of money flows in arriving at what is required for basic financial planning. As you read this example you may find it necessary to refer back to sev-eral previous chapters to refresh your memory on a particular subject. It's all part of the learning process as you develop your particular PLAN in line with our safe and secure investment ideas.

When you construct your own money plan keep in mind that an overall lifetime structure is what you want to achieve—sort of a personal road map for your family's journey. We are trying to erect a series of present and future mile markers so we don't lose our way getting to the ultimate destination of financial in-dependence. Don't get bogged down in the minutiae of too many options. Concentrate on the big-ticket items, and the rest should take care of itself.

There is one place where your plan should be detailed down to the penny. The monthly update of your investment accounts in Quicken and your checkbook are the places where exact amounts are desirable. Completely enter your information from statements and use downloads from institutions whose software works well with Quicken. (Not all do.). The Quicken program will generate very detailed tabulations, which are necessary in a *Net Worth Statement*. On certain occasions, such as applying for a mortgage, you may need to provide your Net Worth Statement to third parties to substantiate your creditworthiness. In that case you must have complete accuracy. But mostly, we are trying to generate direction and purpose in your financial life with an over-riding PLAN. Let's examine a case with that in mind.

EXAMPLE 1:

John and Ginny

John and Ginny are thirty-one years of age, been married four years, and have graduated from excellent colleges with degrees in finance and biochemistry, respectively. They have been working for the past five years. They live in a rented apartment in New York City, where John is employed on Wall Street as an analyst with a base salary of $125,000 per year and Ginny works for a pharmaceutical company in a laboratory and earns $75,000 per year. Ginny was previously married and as part of her divorce settlement will receive $12,000 per year for ten years. John has a yearly bonus that usually is in the range of $50,000 per year if the firm and his department do well. They both have 401(k) plans at work with a 3 percent match by their employer. Their parents have gifted $10,000 to their first child for future college educational expenses and are likely to do the same for each child in their household. They have a three-year-old son named Roger, and Ginny is three months pregnant with their second child. They also have saved $105,000 in investment accounts (all in stocks and mutual funds) and have built up a rainy-day fund of $30,000 (again all in stocks). Their investment account earned a 7 percent return or $7,350 ($105,000 X .07 = $7,350), but those earnings are never touched and not considered income for our PLAN purposes. They are thinking about purchasing a house in the suburbs, since their jobs seem quite secure and a new child is on the way.

THE APPROACH:

As with any financial PLAN, John and Ginny must begin with our core principles of:

1. Develop a PLAN that embodies a *safe and secure approach* and encompasses the most likely future needs that can

be currently identified. Savings are a major component of building a solid base in these difficult and changing times.

2. Create a *consistent increase in available cash flow* by proper budgeting, wise investments, and salary promotion in their jobs.

3. Take charge of their financial life with a serious time commitment to *educated investment execution.* This involves data entry and update on a regular basis.

STEP ONE: WORKSHEETS

In our active planning process, it all starts with the basics of listing in a chart the applications of their income to their current outflow expenses. The first step in the process is to fill in **Chart 1** of **Yearly Income Worksheet Items** and then **Chart 2** of **Expense Worksheet Items** to obtain a clear picture of their present situation. Next, assign categories of fixed, variable, occasional, or capital to their expenses ("**F**","**V**," "**O**," **or** "**C**"). The source information is available from many records including their Quicken laptop program, checkbook(s), receipts they have saved in files, credit card and other statements also in files, and their tax returns.

They do this exercise so that they can see in one place how money flows into and out of their household. It makes visible the **variable expense** items that are within their direct control. Most times, analyzing what is not a **fixed expense** can produce obvious savings and give improved control of their money. If John and Ginny manage their outflow of expenses better, they will increase their excess of unapplied income. This is money they may invest to increase family wealth. We will assume those unapplied funds are contributed to their yearly **capital additions to their portfolio,** and not spent on new items.

Lastly, John and Ginny have selected a savings rate of 25 percent of their **net income** (after all taxes) as their yearly target for capital additions to their financial portfolio. This is an ambitious number compared to their friends, but they understand that the sooner they save (and the larger the amount saved in earlier years) the more wealth will build through the **miracle of compounding**. In our PLAN we treat savings as just another expense and it is a budgeted allocation of net income. In reality it is not an expense in the same way as purchasing a TV, paying rent etc., but a movement from the present year into a long-term portfolio.

– JOHN AND GINNY –
YEARLY INCOME WORKSHEET ITEMS

CHART 1

SOURCE	YEARLY INCOME (BEFORE TAXES)	MONTHLY INCOME	% OF TOTAL INCOME	
John Salary	$ 125,000	$ 10,416	48%	
John 3% 401(k) match	$ 3,750 (1)			Not taxable income
John bonus	$ 50,000		19%	
Ginny Salary	$ 75,000	$ 6,250	29%	
Ginny 3% 401(k) match (1)	$ 2,250 (1)			Not taxable income
Ginny's Alimony	$ 12,000	$ 1,000	4.6%	
Total Gross Income Before Taxes	$262,000	$ 17,666		
Net Income After Taxes (2)	$131,000	$ 10,916		
25% of Net Income To Be Saved (3)	$ 32,750			

(1) Employer 3 percent match portion in their workplace 401(k). We will consider this $6,000 to be income but it is not taxable until with drawn nor is it spendable in the current year. However, it will count as savings in chart 2 below.

(2) Assume for simplicity that the tax burden where John and Ginny live is approximately 50 percent of gross income including Federal, State, and City taxes.

(3) Selected by John and Ginny at 25 percent of net income for their PLAN as their capital addition to investments for the coming year.

– JOHN AND GINNY –
EXPENSE WORKSHEET ITEMS
CHART 2

EXPENSES	YEARLY EXPENSE	MONTHLY EXPENSE	% OF YEARLY EXPENSE(1)	F,V,O,C
Clothing	$ 7,200	$ 600	5.5	V
Food	$ 10,400	$ 867	7.9	V
Rent	$ 30,000	$ 2,500	22.9	F
Utilities	$ 2,400	$ 200	1.8	F
Dental	$ 240	$ 20	.2	F
Charity	$ 3,000	$ 250	2.3	V
Smart Phones/Tablets	$ 2,400	$ 200	1.8	V
Internet +Cable TV	$ 2,400	$ 200	1.8	V
Entertainment	$ 4,800	$ 400	3.7	V
Vacation	$ 8,000	N/A	6.1	V
Auto	$ 6,000	$ 500	4.6	V
Insurance (2)	$ 3,600	$ 300	2.7	F
New Computer	$ 2,600	N/A	2.0	O
New Child Furniture	$ 3,000	N/A	2.3	O
Capital Additions: (3)				
EXPENSES	YEARLY EXPENSE	MONTHLY EXPENSE	% OF YEARLY EXPENSE(1)	F,V,O,C
a. John & Ginny 401k	$6,000	$ 1,500	4.6	C

				C Not an expense item
b. Employer 401(k) match (4)	$6,000	$ 1,500	4.6	C Not an expense item
c. Addition Needed for 25% saved	$20,750	$ 1,729	15.8	C
Total Capital Additions	$32,750			From Chart 1
Health Insurance	$ 3,600	$ 300	2.7	F
Gifts	$ 1,500	N/A	1.1	V
Child care	$ 4,800	$ 400	3.7	F
Net Income After Taxes	$131,000			
Total Expenses	$120,290			

(1) Approximation.

(2) Includes term life ($1 million on John and $500,000 on Ginny), renter's insurance, and auto insurance.

(3) Their chosen savings percent of 25 percent of their net income after taxes computed on Chart 1 ($262,000 X .25) is $32,750. They each save 3 percent of pay, which is deducted from their pay for their 401(k) contribution at work. Together their total is $6,000 per year ($200,000 X .03). This is invested in their 401(k) toward retirement. The balance necessary for a 25 percent saving of net income they chose in their PLAN is $20,750 because their employer matches their $6,000 with an additional $6,000 ($32,750 - $12,000 =$20,750).

(4) Not an expense of John or Ginny but shown here to illustrate they are saving this match amount.

Now let's examine in detail each expense item that has been marked with a "**V**" to see if there are some additional savings they might achieve by changing their behavior.

1. **Clothing:** John and Ginny are young and like nice clothing. They always shop on sale days and purchase good quality garments. They don't want to cut back this item and will leave it as 5.5 percent of their expenses.

2. **Food:** With one child home and another on the way, there is no probable savings on the food expense of 7.9 percent in the coming year.

3. **Charity:** Charity at 2.3 percent is an area for minor savings until such time as their wealth allows more generous contributions.

4. **Smart Phones/Tablets:** Cell phones are part of the culture and both people text friends very often, which explains their high monthly bill. Perhaps they can save a little here with more restraint.

5. **Internet:** Internet and Cable TV are items that help relax these two professionals in the evening so this is not likely to drop to a cheaper plan.

6. **Entertainment:** At 3.7 percent of expenses, entertainment cost is fairly high (at $400 each month) and they could cut back on one evening each month and budget only $300/month. They might replace the evening by taking advantage of lower cost visits to museums, a book or other club, volunteer work, free concerts, or a hundred other ways.

7. **Vacation:** Spending 6.1 percent of yearly income on vacation expense is definitely an area to examine. Once they are financially secure, they can spend at that level or higher.

8. **Auto:** John and Ginny are spending 4.6 percent of their total outlay on an auto expense yet they live in a large city with excellent mass transit. The family only uses a car once or twice a month to visit parents, so it would be much less expensive to rent a car for when they need it.

9. **Gifts:** Gifts are not extraordinary at 1.1 percent of expenses and will remain as noted.

The exercise of reviewing expenses by type each year can have a definite effect on your behavior. When all expenses are laid out in one chart it becomes clear that certain **variable expense** items can be changed by different conduct: some upwards and others changed downwards. Likewise, **occasional expenses** can come under tighter control so perhaps it is possible to postpone purchasing a new computer until next year. **Capital additions** are clearly delineated as an expense, and moving funds out of a yearly budget into investments assures continued growth in the portfolio.

An example of increasing a variable expense is the "**Insurance**" category. Today it reflects a three-person unit with **term life** coverage on John for $1 million. With the arrival of a second child and the family now a four-person unit, it is a good idea to increase John's term life coverage to $2 million or more to provide safety for Ginny. The **term life** coverage of $500,000 on Ginny should also be reviewed and raised to $1 million or more. The difference in their term life policy face amounts reflects their relative income contribution from their careers. In any case, their coverage selections should allow for the care, development, and education of the two children. Premiums will rise accordingly and quotes on the higher coverage amounts from agents (or online vendors) will increase the $3,600 yearly expense now entered in **Chart 2**. They have decided to add disability insurance for a few years because of the large financial commitment required to secure a first house.

Conversely, they will cancel auto insurance and sell their car, which will eliminate part of the $6,000 variable expense from **Chart 2**. However, to properly budget they should add a **new expense category** for "**Rental Cars**" to reflect their outlay when visiting their parents.

STEP TWO: HAM-AND-EGG BUDGET

At this point most of the hard work has been completed for budgeting. John and Ginny's yearly budget is determined from the final results of the two worksheets in Step One. They've altered their behavior on certain variable items. Once all of the information is gathered, analyzed, and totals changed to reflect new behavior, they are ready to prepare this year's **Ham-and-Egg Budget**. All of their income is accounted for and all expenses are entered to produce the final worksheet. Let's review some of the assumptions in their overall **PLAN**:

1. They have chosen to save 25 percent (our target calls for saving 20–50 percent) of their net income. Some sacrifice in consumption in the present year will pay off handsomely in a few years. John and Ginny understand the concept of the **miracle of compounding** and how it builds a better future.

2. Their income level puts them in the highest tax bracket. Their pre-tax income is $262,000 and that means with proper budgeting they can afford many elements in a long-term **PLAN.**

3. John and Ginny recognize they are lucky to each have such a generous employer 401(k) match. Most matches are in the range of 1—3 percent and their employers are near the top of the range.

4. They have already accumulated $105,000 of savings in investment accounts (over five years of employment including one year when they were not married and had lower expenses), which generated a 7 percent return this year and contributed $7,350 of asset growth to their **net worth.** Remember, in our **PLAN** earnings on investments are always saved so they may compound over time. They are never spent as yearly expenses.

5. After they complete the worksheets of **Chart 1** and **Chart 2**, their Ham-and-Egg Budget will show how much of their net income will be an **excess of net income over their expenses.** The next question is what to do with the excess.

– JOHN AND GINNY –
HAM-AND-EGG BUDGET

CHART 3
(for the year ending   /   /   )

INCOME	YEARLY TOTAL	COMMENTS
1. Fixed Income		
John Salary	$125,000	
John Bonus	$ 50,000	
Ginny	$ 75,000	
Alimony	$ 12,000	Six years to run
TOTAL INCOME	$262,000	
a. **Total Spendable Income**	$131,000	Net after tax
Other Income	$ 7,350	Investment income (from $105,000 of savings)- left to compound
2. Fixed Expenses		
Rent	$ 30,000	
Utilities	$ 2,400	
Dental	$ 240	
Insurance (1)	$ 3,000	
Health Insurance	$ 3,600	
Child Care	$ 4,800	
TOTAL	$ 70,790	
3. Variable Expenses		
Clothing	$ 7,200	
Food	$ 10,400	
Charity(2)	$ 2,500	
Smart Phones/Tablets	$ 2,400	
Internet + Cable	$ 2,400	
INCOME	**YEARLY TOTAL**	**COMMENTS**

Entertainment(3)	$ 3,600	
Vacation(4)	$ 6,000	
Auto	Eliminated	
Rental Cars	$ 2,400	
Gifts	$ 1,500	
TOTAL	$ 40,900	
4. Occasional Expenses(5)		
Last year's amount	$ 5,600	
Misc. New Baby	$ 3,000	
New Video Camera	$ 1,000	
House hunting Expense	$ 2,000	
TOTAL	$ 11,600	
5. Capital Additions		
401(k) Contributions	$ 6,000 (6)	
Additional Savings During Year	$ 20,750	
a. **TOTAL EXPENSES**	$123,290	
b. **EXCESS OF INCOME OVER EXPENSES**	$ 7,710	**A minus B = C**

(1) Reflects removal of auto insurance and additional term life insurance on John and Ginny as well as disability insurance on each of them. Note the total amount has decreased even with new term life and disability because auto was the largest component.

(2) Cut from $3,000 to $2,500, anticipating baby and purchasing a house.

(3) Cut from $400 to $300 per month.

(4) Cut from $8,000 to $6,000.

(5) Kept last year's level, plus some anticipated new items this year.

(6) The employer match to their 401(k) is not their expense. Only their contributions are in the budget.

John and Ginny have completed assembling a workable budget for their income level that incorporates the expense elements of their family's life. It will be a useful tool for the coming year. A year from now they will do the exercise again and see how closely they came to their expectations with only a few hours of effort. They have taken a major step toward control of their financial management.

STEP THREE: WHIPPED-CREAM-AND-CHERRY BUDGET

John and Ginny know they want to incorporate into their planning some major anticipated life changes. That is precisely the purpose of the **Whipped-Cream-and-Cherry Budget.** It is really identical to the Ham-and-Egg Budget of **Chart 3** with the exception of adding specific recognition (with a separate investment account) and funding for **future goals**. These are most likely to be events such as the purchase of a home; sending Roger and their other siblings to college (and possibly graduate school); funding a desire for worldwide travel; owning a ski condo at their favorite resort: and of course their own retirement planning. These other goals may be funded each year from **capital additions** as well as **an excess of income over expenses.** In this year's Ham-and-Egg Budget there is $7,710 of money that can be committed to fund future events that are presently identifiable by John and Ginny.

There are two ways of providing financial support for the future, but they can have a distinction. When a **future goal** is funded from **excess income over expense** it is usually a **shorter** period before the money needs to be spent. So for example, renovation to a new house or additional down payment might be funded by excess income over expense without waiting many years for compounding to grow the money. On the other hand, **college** for an infant is many years away and **retirement** is still further. These are future goals that are funded out of portfolios comprised of capital additions that have benefited from the miracle of long periods of compounding.

This is a logical way to approach a PLAN because having an excess of income over expense means that the chosen savings percentage for the year (here 25 percent of net income) has been met and there is still income left over. Of course, an alternative is to simply consider the excess income over expenses in any year as a **supplemental capital addition** to the entire portfolio ($32,750 + $7,710 = $40,460), which raises the savings goal from 25 percent to 31 percent this year.

– JOHN AND GINNY –
FUTURE GOALS

CHART 4
WHIPPED-CREAM-AND-CHERRY BUDGET
(as of   /   /   )

FUTURE GOAL	YEARLY $ NEEDED	TOTAL $ TO GOAL	YEARS TO GOAL
1. Purchasing First House			
2. Roger's College			
3. New baby's college			
4. Around the World Vacation			

1. PURCHASING FIRST HOUSE

The decision to build a family often comes with a decision to purchase a first house. This is such a large economic decision for most people that some of the rules in the PLAN may need to be delayed for it to transpire. Our PLAN considers equity in a house as part of a financial portfolio (and safer than owning stocks or mutual funds). Home equity has a return in the appreciation of real estate (if that happens), and the benefit of providing comfortable shelter. Let's look at this important decision with John and Ginny. (Once again we will ignore brokerage commissions and other purchase/sale expenses for simplicity.)

First, there is the matter of purchasing a house in which their monthly mortgage payments build equity, rather than simply paying rent. They have $105,000 in investment accounts and a net after-tax monthly income of $10,916. They are good candidates for home ownership and most lenders would find them very attractive customers. Our usual rule of thumb in our **PLAN** is that a down payment should be 25 percent of the purchase price, but that would limit them to a house in the range of $420,000 (.25 X $420,000 = $105,000). In the area they live, a nice four-bedroom home in a community with good schools that is within commuting distance for their jobs is likely to cost in the range of $500-650,000. What to do?

DOWN PAYMENT AMOUNTS

PRICE OF HOUSE	25% DOWN	20% DOWN	15% DOWN
$420,000	$105,000	$84,000	$63,000
$520,000	$130,000	$104,000	$78,000
$620,000	$155,000	$124,000	$93,000

John and Ginny believe they can find a house that would work for them for $550,000. They feel that they are willing to commit three-quarters of their investment portfolio of $105,000, which is now in stocks and mutual funds, into the equity of their home. In addition, they will use $15,000 of the $20,750 that will be a budget line item of **capital additions** this year from their Ham-and-Egg Budget as well as all of their **excess of income over expenses** of $7,710. They total this and see their available cash down payment will be $101,460 ($78,750 + $15,000 + $7,710 = $101,460). They will then need to calculate their monthly mortgage payment (excluding real estate tax escrow required by many lenders).

MONTHLY MORTGAGE PAYMENT

PRICE OF HOUSE	DOWN PAYMENT	MORTGAGE AMOUNT	DOWN PAYMENT PERCENTAGE	MONTHLY MORTGAGE (1)
$500,000	$100,000	$400,000	20%	$2,026
$550,000	$100,000	$450,000	18.2%	$2,246
$600,000	$100,000	$500,000	16.7%	$2,532

(1) These numbers come from the Google mortgage calculator. APR rate 4.498 percent. Thirty-year fixed. No points.

John and Ginny assume they will qualify for a thirty-year, fixed-rate mortgage, with no points at the prevailing **annual percentage rate (APR)**. Then they go to www.google.com or www.bing.com and locate one of the many **mortgage calculators** and fill in their information (18.2 percent down payment) to determine that at the present time, and at the currently offered APR (4.498 percent), their monthly mortgage payment amount will be $2,246 on a house that costs $550,000. This is less than their nondeductible monthly rent ($2,500). The interest portion of their mortgage will be a deduction on their tax return and will increase their net after-tax income. The principle portion will pay down the loan a little each year. You can get a schedule of this breakdown for each of the thirty years on most mortgage calculators. (I will not deal with real estate taxes John and Ginny will have to pay, nor with upkeep. These are not known until a specific property is selected.)

John and Ginny decide that when they buy a home with a down payment less than 25 percent (here 18.2

percent) they will make up the difference ($37,400 in our example) over the next ten years. They return to www.google.com or www.bing.com and find a **present value calculator,** which will tell them how much they should budget each year to have saved $37,400 in ten years (to complete a 25 percent down payment). In any case, the approach of a modified lower down payment is still *safe and secure* because:

1. They have not touched their **rainy-day fund.**
2. Their income and jobs are reasonably secure.
3. Their monthly **mortgage payment** is not a major step up from their rent.
4. They are still funding their **retirement** though their 401(k) plans.

Note: The above example of a first house purchase has many different parts to it that occur over time and have been left out for simplicity. For example, the value of their house could well appreciate to $750,000 during the next ten years in which case John and Ginny would have $300,000 of equity in a $750,000 house. That would be 40 percent equity, and they might decide they no longer need to budget to increase their equity in the house over the original down payment. If, in a few years, they decide to trade up or down to a new house, the dynamics of their equity and terms of their mortgage will change. John and Ginny can only produce the best PLAN that is clear to them at the moment. (It is the same for you.)

2. COLLEGE FOR ROGER AND THE NEW BABY

John and Ginny will need a PLAN for Roger's college tuition and the new baby's as well. They assume that college begins at eighteen years of age and so there are fifteen more years for three-year-old Roger to start college and eighteen more years until he finishes a four-year degree. There are eighteen more years for the newborn to start college and twenty-one years until the completion of a four-year degree. They will make assumptions on the earning rate on their investments, the type and cost of college chosen, and once again use the tools on the Internet. At www.google.com or www.bing.com there are many calculators that perform a **future value calculation** to determine the likely future tuition cost in fifteen and eighteen years. They will need to budget a yearly amount in their **PLAN** to handle these future expenses.

In their family's case, parents have given Roger $10,000 to be placed in his college fund. We know that the sooner money is invested and allowed to undergo the miracle of compounding, the greater the future effect. John and Ginny can invest the $10,000 in **zero-coupon bonds** with an interest rate of 4percent and choose to place Roger's $10,000 in a ladder (see "Bond Ladders" in Chapter 7) of $2,500 each in years fifteen to eighteen. The bonds will mature in each of the four years, and their payout may be applied toward the yearly tuition bills. Assuming the same gift is made for the newborn, a zero-coupon bond structure would work there as well. Over time, John and Ginny or their parents will make more additions to each child's college fund, which will produce a greater total to be available to meet the college cost.

3. AROUND THE WORLD VACATION

John and Ginny have always wanted to travel extensively around the world. They realize that at the present moment they have careers and are beginning to raise a family. However, in twenty-two years, when the newborn is out of college, they intend to take a year off and just travel wherever their hearts lead them. After speaking with several travel agents and reviewing a book by someone who actually did it, they estimate that they will need $50,000 **present value** to do what they want. Once again they will return to the Internet and find a **future value calculator**. By now they know the drill. They assume a 3 percent inflation rate. At a 3 percent rate for twenty-two years in the future they will need $95,805(i) for the trip. They will begin to budget accordingly once their house purchase project is complete. This year there are no funds for this goal.

(i)From TCalc online financial calculator at http://tcalc.timevalue.com

STEP FOUR: NET WORTH = PERSONAL BALANCE SHEET

The final exercise in our **PLAN** is the construction of a yearly **Net Worth Statement**. Once they complete it, John and Ginny will have a useful tool for determining how they are doing in meeting their lifetime financial **PLAN**. This quantitative summary of the family's financial condition is a snapshot good only for a specific point in time. Sometimes lenders require this sort of information to determine the ratio of liabilities (debt) a borrower currently has in relation to assets.

Now that John and Ginny have a good handle on their money flows in Quicken, in budgets, and other financial records, it should not be an overly complex matter to use the information to fill in their Net Worth Statement.

– JOHN AND GINNY –

NET WORTH STATEMENT
(as of   /   /   )

CHART 5

ASSETS	VALUE
Checking Account	$ 2,670
Investment Accounts	$105,000
Rainy Day Account	$ 30,000
Vehicle	$ 8,750
401(k) Plan John	$ 31,250
401(k) Plan Ginny	$ 30,330
Roger College Fund	$ 10,000
Household effects	$ 5,000
TOTAL ASSETS	$223,000
LIABILITIES	
Health Insurance Qtr Payment	$900
Credit Card Monthly Balance	$671
TOTAL LIABILITIES	$1,571
NET WORTH	$221,429

EXAMPLE 2:

Art and Judy

Art and Judy are forty-two and thirty-nine years old respectively, have been married sixteen years, and have two children: Lisa (age fourteen) and Maggie (age sixteen). For the last twelve years Art has been employed by an advertising agency and has worked his way up from entry-level office staff (an annual salary of $55,000) to vice president (an annual salary of $200,000). Judy worked for the first six years of their marriage as a paralegal at a law firm earning $65,000 annually, but has chosen to stay at home for the last four years.

During the last five years the family has lived in a home that cost $650,000, which they bought with a 5 percent down payment ($32,500) and financed with a five-year, adjustable-rate mortgage, on a thirty year repayment schedule, at the lowest interest rate then available of 6.2 percent. After the initial five-year period, their mortgage principle balance of $617,500 will reset its interest at market rates. Interest rates have declined in the last four years and are currently 4.6 percent for a similar mortgage.

*They have managed to save only $90,000 during their ten-year marriage (says above married sixteen years) after their house down payment. It was invested by a broker in "growth stocks," but three years ago Art decided that real estate values could only continue rising and he invested $50,000 of their savings toward the purchase of a five-unit commercial strip mall that was fully rented and had a purchase price of $1 million. Art and Judy personally guaranteed a fifteen-year loan in the principal amount of $950,000, which was at a fixed 7 percent interest rate and had monthly payments of $8,538. The mortgage was offset by **rental income** of $11,250 from the five* units (each rented at $2,250 per month). After all expenses (property tax, repairs, gardening, snow removal, insurance, legal, electric, etc.) the commercial strip mall provided **positive cash flow** of $1,500 per month. This income is fully sheltered by the **depreciation** deduction on the strip mall so Art and Judy recognized no taxable income. They spent the $1,500 each month on two new luxury automobiles.

In their own minds, Art and Judy believe they have set aside $10,000 for Lisa and $15,000 for Maggie out of their savings of $90,000, toward college expenses. They have not placed the money in their children's names and still maintain it within their own investment brokerage account.

In 2008, the economy went into a major recession and several things transpired. First, a restaurant in the strip mall went bankrupt because of slower business, and stopped paying rent. Second, Maggie decided she wanted to go to an Ivy League college. She had the necessary grades and the support of her high school guidance counselor. Third, the real estate value of their home dropped significantly; the cost of a similar house is now in the range of $575–$600,000. Fourth, several major clients at the advertising firm reduced their ad budgets and all employees took a 10 percent salary cut. Art's take-home pay is now $8,000 a month.

Let's examine the impact on Art and Judy and their family:

1. Before the recession, their commercial building was providing about $1,500 per month in tax-sheltered **positive cash flow** over and above expense. With one of the five units in the strip mall empty, and no prospect of being rented anytime soon, they are in a bind. Their monthly rental income is now $9,000 ($11,250- $2,250 = $9,000). The $9,000 just barely covers the monthly mortgage of $8,538.

Art had his accountant calculate the monthly expenses of the strip mall to be approximately $1,212 per month. Art and Judy now are faced with a **shortfall** of $750 each month for the expenses. They arrive at this amount by taking the reduced rental income of $9,000 minus the $8,538 mortgage payment to leave $462 per month. The balance needed to cover $1,212 of expenses is $750 and they must provide this from the $20,000 of investment accounts remaining after buying the strip mall. This is a dangerous situation because if a second unit becomes vacant, they will be in serious trouble.

Their current problems with the strip mall could have been avoided by:

   a. Choosing a **smaller** size real estate investment in relation to their down payment ability.

   b. Choosing a more **liquid** investment than real estate (bond, ETF, mutual fund, etc.).

   c. Saving the $18,000 per year positive cash flow during the last three years in an investment account, which would have provided **$54,000 of cushion** for rental shortfalls, expenses, and possible upgrades to the property.

2. Maggie may wish to go to an Ivy League college, but the savings Art and Judy have put away are wholly inadequate to cover even the first year's tuition. Maggie probably will not qualify for a financial-aid scholarship because of Art's income level, so it looks like poor planning will thwart her dreams. She needs to investigate state schools, student loans, and merit scholarships and get part-time work to start saving for college.

3. Art's gross monthly salary has now been reduced by 10 percent. His take-home pay after taxes is approxi-

mately $8,000. Once their mortgage payment of $3,782 is made, it leaves $4,218 for all other expenses. Their house is far too expensive in relation to their original down payment and current income. Using our rule of thumb of 25 percent, they should have had something close to $162,500 of equity when they purchased their home, rather than $32,500. Their **loan to equity ratio** is calculated below:

Loan ($617,500)/ Equity ($32,500) = 5.3

They have more than $5 of debt for every dollar of equity in their house and that makes it too **highly leveraged.** Their monthly mortgage payment of $3,782 is approximately 47 percent of Art's reduced income of $8,000 ($3,782/$8,000 = .47). That leaves a little more than $4,000 to cover all other expenses and to build some savings.

Some additional points:

4. Art and Judy have **no rainy-day fund,** and that is a serious overall mistake in our safe and secure **PLAN.** They need to increase their savings and decrease their expenses to fund one.

5. **Their mortgage will reset this year.** They are fortunate that rates have dropped from their original 6.2 percent to a lower level. Today they are 4.6 percent as calculated under their mortgage note for the next five years. The reset will decrease their monthly mortgage payment from approximately $3,782 per month to $3,467 per month. That extra $315 each month can go toward the $750 expenses of the strip mall not covered by rental income.

WHAT IS THE PLAN FOR THE FUTURE?

1. Art and Judy need to enter all of their records into Quicken, set up a file system, list all their sources of income, list all their expenses, create a Ham-and-Egg Budget, construct a Whipped-Cream-and-Cherry Budget, and realistically look at their Net Worth Statement. This exercise will lead to several obvious lifestyle changes that can still make them wealthy. They have twenty-three or more years before retirement so the miracle of compounding can work for them with a little sacrifice.

2. The first **behavioral change** may fall on Judy. She needs to return to the workforce to bolster the family finances. In a recession there may be fewer jobs and she may also discover that her skills have become rusty. Still, the family needs more income and her contribution at this critical juncture is important. Most of her income should be directed into **retirement savings in safe and secure bonds** and also to **bolster college accounts** for Lisa and Maggie.

3. As soon as the housing market recovers, Art and Judy should look to **replace their home** with a more modest one. The family's spending pattern needs to move into line with income. In four years both girls will be out of the house and that is an ideal time to downsize. If the market recovers sooner, they should make this move then.

4. The **strip mall is an inappropriate investment** for Art and Judy so once it is again fully rented they should place it on the market. All positive **cash flow in excess of expenses** in the future should be saved in a special account as a buffer for any changes in the tenant structure.

5. The two luxury cars must go immediately to stop the monthly payments. Once again, behavior changes will

bring about more modest transportation that should work just as well.

6. Art and Judy should begin in earnest a **rainy-day fund** with money each month. In our **PLAN** we save 20–50 percent of net income and this means they should be saving at least $1,600 each month. Their disposable income after mortgage payments is $4,218 so deducting their **savings expense** they will have $2,618 per month for living expenses. With a tightly followed budget holding their spending behavior in line, they should do well on that sum.

7. The money that Art and Judy have dedicated for college for the girls ($25,000) should be placed in their names in separate accounts. The girls will be in a much lower tax bracket and this will also ensure that if Art and Judy get in financial trouble the funds will not be touched to settle parental financial affairs.

Improper financial planning has placed this family in a highly undesirable situation that should have been avoided. Had Art and Judy concentrated on saving more of their income sooner, chosen a more modest house, not invested in a large piece of commercial real estate without a more substantial net worth (with liquid assets to cushion problems), and followed the steps in *The Money Plan* their lives and stress levels would be much improved. It is still not too late for them to recover and do a reasonably good job of producing financial security and wealth. The recession will prove to be a wake-up call, and now that they are using *The Money Plan* together, with behavioral modifications everything should turn out well.

EXAMPLE 3:

Mary

Mary is a thirty-four-year-old single professional making a $95,000 salary and living in the Pacific Northwest. She has worked for the last six years in a start-up software company that recently went public and that has given her a substantial nest egg. In her financial life Mary has only a vague idea of what she should do, and although she is very computer literate she does not know how to use Quicken or any financial program. She reads all of the computer magazines but not much else except for romance novels. Her portfolio consists of $2 million in Snoogle Inc. stock, a $20,000 rainy-day fund, a brokerage account with $35,000 in high-tech stocks that she leaves in the discretion of a broker, and a $250,000 condominium that she purchased with a $35,000 down payment and a fifteen-year 6.75 percent mortgage. Her parents are also professionals with an excellent net worth, but her brother is twenty-eight years old and has suffered for many years from a motorcycle accident that left him partially paralyzed.

The recent recession has not harmed Snoogle Inc. or its product, which appeals to a student market. Her condominium was worth $500,000 two years ago but is now worth only $350,000. It could use a newer kitchen, which would cost about $10,000. Mary has dated several men in the last few years but at the moment there is no one special in her life. At some point in the future Mary would like to travel for a year and study French.

WHAT IS THE PLAN FOR THE FUTURE?

1. Mary needs to take responsibility for her individual financial **PLAN**. Although she has been very successful so

far it is possible for her to suffer a sharp reversal because so much of her assets are out of her control.

2. It is critical for her to have some understanding of the markets and financial matters so Mary should begin reading *The Wall Street Journal*, *Bloomberg Business Week*, *Forbes*, and an investment letter such as *Marketimer*.

3. Mary's main asset is a portfolio of Snoogle Inc. stock worth $2 million, but its value may not go linearly upward. If the value should rise to $4 million it will not significantly change her life, except that perhaps she could drink very fancy wines. However, if the value of Snoogle Inc. stock should go to $0 and the company collapse it will significantly and negatively impact Mary's financial life. She has **failed to diversify** sufficiently and follow our safe and secure PLAN as she is too closely tied to the fortunes of her employer. Even if Mary has some restrictions on her shares, there are still techniques to diversify and begin assembling a **bond ladder.** It is possible to work within these restrictions using a specialized service available from major brokerage firms and many law firms for a fee. Proper **diversity** is definitely worth the expense.

4. The down payment on Mary's condominium should have been $62,500 to meet our **25 percent test,** but she only put down $35,000 (14 percent). However, even in the current depressed market this property has a value of $350,000 so she actually has 38 percent equity ($100,000 + $35,000 divided by $350,000). She might be better off directing her savings into her Whipped-Cream-and-Cherry Budget **Future Goals** (for a year off and a new kitchen) as well as **retirement.** The younger she is when she saves for the future, the longer the period for the miracle of compounding to build her wealth.

5. Mary's mortgage is at 6.75 percent, on a fifteen-year schedule for $215,000, which plugged into the **Google mortgage calculator** produces a $1,902 monthly payment. Rates have dropped and Mary will be better off obtaining a thirty-year mortgage at a current fixed rate of 4.75 percent to reduce her payment to $1,121 per month. She will then have $781 more to invest each month.

6. Mary has given discretion to a broker over her other investment portfolio and those funds were invested in high tech. That means high risk. She needs to take direct control of her finances and make less risky choices.

7. Finally, Mary may wish to help her parents establish a **trust** for her brother to help him along in case he is unable to work. With a trust he can be provided with a basic floor of income but he will not be able to spend the core amount of the trust. A good lawyer or accountant can give advice in this area.

Overall, Mary can be in very good shape, moving toward a goal of financial security, independence, and wealth. However, she should convert her early good fortune in Snoogle Inc. stock to a long-term **PLAN**. She must take responsibility for proper records, diversification, and provision for future items that she considers important in her life. Early success is no assurance of continuing success without the proper pieces put in place.

6

HOW TO SAVE

"If you would be wealthy, think of saving as well as getting."
–BENJAMIN FRANKLIN

You may believe this section is about a trip to a department or electronics store the day after Christmas for the big sales. It's not. Well … that is not entirely true as what you saved by buying on sale can be considered as income and is available to add to savings. From the time I started working until today, my family has always saved and invested 20–50 percent of our total income (earned income plus investment income). And we started saving as early and as much as possible.

It's hard to live in the United States and bring the desire for the latest fad or novelty product into line with the long-term benefit of savings. All of our television and print media is designed to push consumption and accommodate buying with little or no money down. Sometimes politicians cast spending in the light of a patriotic duty. That said, it is much easier than people believe to reflect on whether the greater benefit comes from additions to savings, or depreciating material goods.

Our financial **PLAN** is firmly in the camp of living well while emphasizing the virtue of contributing additional dollars to financial growth. We also emphasize *safe and secure* in our **PLAN** so the **rainy-day fund** is the first and most important element of savings, once you understand some methods for making savings part of your everyday financial life. Money saved and placed in investments means more money out later in life. Much more!

Think of our **PLAN** as a kind of fitness manual for your money that starts with putting aside for the future. The more you save and invest wisely, the larger will be your reward. Constantly adding savings will make life better for you and your family.

THE SAVING 20–50 PERCENT HABIT

This is the most difficult part of our **PLAN** because most people are addicted to spending all they earn ... and then some. Yet the core essence of savings is that your funds, properly invested, will work constantly so you won't have to. Understanding this principle is key to unlocking the power in investment compounding. It's time to break an unhealthy addiction to spending and face the reality that you want to make the future better for you and your family. Who would have thought that we would be quoting P. T. Barnum on this subject, but I can't say it any better myself. Let the content of this quote resonate in your mind for a minute:

> A penny here, and a dollar there, placed at interest, goes on
> accumulating, and in this way the desired result is attained. It
> requires some training, perhaps, to accomplish this economy, but
> when once used to it, you will find there is more satisfaction in
> rational saving than in irrational spending.
> –*THE ART OF MONEY GETTING*, BY P. T. BARNUM

Don't think that it can't be done, because it most assuredly can. But it is difficult at first to acquire the discipline. All you have to do is pretend that you earn 20–50 percent less money and sock the saving part of income away by adding it to your investment portfolio. Then construct your budget from the spendable portion of earned income.

Most of the time what my family managed to save out of our total income was closer to 50 percent. It became easier and easier as our investments began to generate income. We saved 100 percent of our investment income and kept reinvesting it as opposed to spending our profits on current consumption. As our investment portfolio became larger and larger, it accounted for more and more of our savings. At some point your investment earnings are likely to surpass your earnings from your job. The more investment income, the easier it is to hit our 20–50 percent target. In the very beginning, that is not the case, so your family will have to work harder on savings. But money put aside in earlier years is a powerful wealth-building engine. Here are some simple tricks to help your savings **PLAN** work:

1. When you buy something on sale, pretend you paid the retail price and put the difference into your savings.
2. Set up automatic withdrawal for savings of a set amount from your paycheck each month, so the money you receive to spend is lessened. Learn to live on the amount you receive.
3. If you take several vacations each year make one of them a driving vacation rather than a plane flight.
4. Consider doing some of the home renovations you have in mind yourself. It can be made into a family project involving everyone. There will be increased satisfaction and pride in the end result, it will teach your children something about working with their hands, and the cost will be lower. Do-it-yourself has always been a big part of my family's savings **PLAN**.
5. Give your children responsibility for routine maintenance items such as cutting grass, weeding, shoveling

snow, etc. and pay them for doing it. Then have them save their earnings.

6. Postpone purchases to the appropriate sale times. For example, if it was close to Labor Day and my family needed a new TV, we would wait for the Labor Day circulars. If you look at the calendar, there is a major retail promotion in almost every period of the year. (See Money Commandment XIII.)

7. Buy cars in August when new models are coming out and dealers need to move old inventory to make room for the new. Most often the changes from year to year are minor and you can save thousands by accepting a vehicle still on the lot. Then pretend you bought the car earlier in the model year and put the "saved" money in your investment account.

8. Negotiate prices. Ask for discounts or increased savings on big-ticket items. You will be surprised how often you will be accommodated. My favorite advice to my family has been, "What you can talk for you don't have to work for."

Don't get the idea that savings at this high level meant my family did without in suffering silence. While we ate at the horn of plenty our whole lives, sometimes it required restraint and good timing. Most of the larger items and a majority of the common goods we purchased on sale or in bulk at big-box merchandisers like Costco, Sam's Club, and BJs. Often we searched for floor samples, but always for the highest-quality goods at the best prices. When you buy quality, it lasts. If you get quality on sale, there is a double benefit of up-front cost saving and durability.

Over time the miracle of compounding slowly increases your investment income. The earlier you start, the more powerful this tool becomes. Albert Einstein called compounding "the greatest mathematical discovery of all time." There are numerous Web sites to convince you of the value of compounding, and if you need some solid pushing to save, read a few of them. There is also the **Rule of 72** to provide you an easy reference point for quick determination of how a bond, mutual fund, or stock will work for you.

DOUBLING MONEY USING THE RULE OF 72

WHEN YOU MULTIPLY the number of years by which money doubles at a specified rate of interest, the result is always approximately seventy-two. So nine years at 8 percent interest equals seventy-two; twelve years at 6 percent interest is seventy-two; and so forth. This can be expressed as a simple formula to arrive at number of years or a needed interest rate to double money.

$$\text{Interest Rate} = \frac{72}{\text{Number of Years}}$$

$$\text{Number of Years} = \frac{72}{\text{Interest Rate}}$$

Understanding this trick and using the Rule of 72 will make it simple to estimate how long it will take to double your investment or what return your investment requires to meet a stated dollar amount goal. You can also find a calculator for the Rule of 72 at www.moneychimp.com/features/rule72.htm if that is easier. This quick method is fairly accurate on interest rates of up to 20 percent, which will cover most of our safe and secure choices.

There is no better time to start having compounding work for you than today.

Chart 6.1 Will Give You An Excellent Picture Of How Powerful Compounding Is In Your Financial Life.

1. It shows that Investor **B** started saving early at nineteen years of age and only made seven yearly contributions of $2,000.

2. Investor **A** delayed starting saving by only six years, to age twenty-six, and then diligently contributed $2,000 a year for forty years.

3. At age sixty-five, Investor **B** had more total money than Investor **A** even though Investor **B** had only made seven savings contributions versus forty for Investor **A**.

4. The longer-term compounding of money (in *Chart 6.1* at 10 percent) grew Investor B's funds **sixty-six fold** and only grew Investor A's funds **eleven fold. You should now be convinced that** *time and compounding* **are your best financial friends.**

CHART 6.1

COMPARISON OF COMPOUNDING EFFECT FOR A & B INVESTORS WHO CONTRIBUTE TO A PLAN AT DIFFERENT TIMES*(1)

AGE	INVESTOR A CONTRIBUTION	YEAR END VALUE	INVESTOR B CONTRIBUTION	YEAR-END VALUE
8	0	0	0	0
9	0	0	0	0
10	0	0	0	0
11	0	0	0	0
12	0	0	0	0
13	0	0	0	0
14	0	0	0	0
15	0	0	0	0
16	0	0	0	0
17	0	0	0	0
18	0	0	0	0
19	0	0	2,000	2,200
20	0	0	2,000	4,620
21	0	0	2,000	7,282
22	0	0	2,000	10,210
23	0	0	2,000	13,431
24	0	0	2,000	16,974
25	0	0	2,000	20,872
26	2,000	2,200	0	22,959
27	2,000	4,620	0	25,255
28	2,000	7,282	0	27,780
29	2,000	10,210	0	30,558
30	2,000	13,431	0	33,014
31	2,000	16,974	0	36,976
32	2,000	20,872	0	40,673
33	2,000	25,159	0	44,741
34	2,000	29,875	0	49,215
35	2,000	35,062	0	54,136
36	2,000	40,769	0	59,550
37	2,000	47,045	0	65,505
38	2,000	53,950	0	72,055
39	2,000	61,545	0	79261
40	2,000	69,899	0	87,187
41	2,000	79,089	0	95,905
42	2,000	89,198	0	105,496
43	2,000	100,318	0	116,045
44	2,000	112,550	0	127,650
45	2,000	126,005	0	140,415
46	2,000	140,805	0	154,456
47	2,000	157,086	0	169,902
48	2,000	174,995	0	186,892
49	2,000	194,694	0	205,581
50	2,000	216,364	0	226,140
51	2,000	240,200	0	248,754
52	2,000	266,420	0	273,629
53	2,000	295,262	0	300,992
54	2,000	326,988	0	331,091
55	2,000	361,887	0	364,200
56	2,000	400,276	0	400,620
57	2,000	442,503	0	440,682
58	2,000	488,953	0	484,750
59	2,000	540,049	0	533,225
60	2,000	596,254	0	586,548
61	2,000	658,079	0	645,203
62	2,000	726,087	0	709,695
63	2,000	800,896	0	780,695
64	2,000	883,185	0	858,765
65	2,000	973,704	0	944,641

Less Total Invest		**(80,000)**		**(14,000)**
Equals Net Earnings		**893,704**		**930,641**
Money Grew:		**11-fold**		**66-fold**

*Using a constant contribution amount of $2,000 in each yearly investment.

Source: This chart is sourced from an original study by Market Logic of Ft. Lauderdale, FL, and has appeared in Richard Russell's "Wisdom: Rich Man Poor Man," which was posted on the web by Drizzt on July 9, 2006. Mr. Russell has been writing letters on market theory since 1958 and his work is an excellent reference source for money matters.

The lesson here is START SAVING EARLY IN YOUR CAREER. As early and as much as possible. Just as with present and future value formulas, the Internet has many free sites where you can insert numbers and calculate a compounding result. The largest library of formulas I have used is at www.CompoundingToday.com. This is not an exercise you need to do on a regular basis. *Your job is to save 20–50 percent of your earnings and to continue to reinvest as close to 100 percent of your investment earnings as possible.*

PRACTICE MAKES PERFECT (ALMOST)

IF YOU CHOOSE to use banks for savings, check out www. MoneyAisle.com. The site lists more than one hundred federally insured banks that would just love to have your money. All you have to do is enter the amount you want to save in a high-yield savings account or CD and the banks will bid for the funds. It's an easy way to get a feel for the market and there is no obligation to accept any offer. The competition is likely to get you above-average rates with a minimal amount of effort. Use common sense and make certain they have the requisite federal insurance on your funds, as well as an established track record.

I also like www.feedthepig.org for under-savers who need a really fun and useful push to save. Once you visit FeedthePig.com, I'm pretty sure you will use it in some way.

These Web sites are hardly substitutes for your PLAN, but they can supplement what you are trying to accomplish.

RAIN, RAIN, GO AWAY

They say that sh*t usually happens just after someone has mucked out the pony's stable. It's true—just ask any horse owner. This analogy snaps us back to the task of preparing for the imperfections that go on in everyone's life. Usually, there is no apparent reason for the curveball we have been thrown, and we probably could not have anticipated it. Car accidents are just that, disease rarely leaves a calling card, natural disaster is decisively eco-unfriendly, and sometimes you are the tiny bug and not the windshield. What we can do is recognize that there are imponderables out there in life ... and prepare to meet them successfully.

Our **PLAN** is partially based on a basic building block consisting of a minimum of six months of a liquid *rainy-day fund*. It should be your first savings goal. As with our Money Commandment IX (don't carry credit card balances), there is little compromise in our **PLAN** on this rainy-day subject. You should have six, or even better nine, months of cash in a money market fund or other highly liquid investment (Treasuries, etc.) that would cover most of your basic expenses if the unthinkable becomes a reality. As your financial and family life grows more complex, the amount you have in this untouchable pocketbook should increase. It is essential to look at this number and review it every few months to assure its adequacy. The rainy-day fund is the best sleeping pill ever invented, and a big step in the direction of financial security.

Your rainy-day fund should exist outside of all other assets. Our **PLAN** does not worry that these funds earn a lower short-term interest rate and are not the best place to park large investments. A secondary benefit to our rainy-day fund is that it is our self-actuated insurance. This money should not be invested for the long term or raided for buying a home, sending the kids to college, or any other cash need. It is there so if you lose your job, there is no undue pressure to accept a position you don't really want. It is there so if an auto accident causes a stack of medical bills, you are not further stressed by meeting daily expenses during your recovery. It is there as a safety net for you and your family. It is every prudent person's first order of business to establish a rainy-day fund as soon as you begin your work life.

SECURED LENDING IS USEFUL ON A RAINY DAY

THE RAINY-DAY FUND may be the standout exception to our general aversion to borrowing. If you have plenty of equity in a safe asset like a home, part of the rainy-day fund can be in the form of a line of credit that can be tapped under all circumstances, for up to *half* of the fund. Be aware that many credit lines have a clause that makes them completely inaccessible if you have a change of circumstance. Check out the terms of any credit line you want to use as half your rainy-day fund to be sure it is absolutely available no matter what transpires so long as the asset securing it is still valuable collateral. But you should still want half of the money in liquid assets because borrowing takes time and, in some emergencies, you may not have that luxury. Cash in a money market is immediate and certain. Your rainy-day fund and its half-cash requirement is the cornerstone of your safe and secure philosophy.

CASH FLOW LEADS TO THE LAND OF MILK AND HONEY

Recall the metaphor of our *PLAN* as a three-legged stool comfortably holding up our financial bum. The first leg of the stool is the notion of **safe and secure**. The second leg is **consistent increase**

of available cash flow. For a company, the common definition of **free cash flow** is:

Cash receipts − Cash payments = Free cash flow

In other words, it is the movement of cash in and out of the company, taking into account the timing of when bills need to be paid. If a bill is due and a company has no cash to pay it, then it may go out of business. So *how much* cash and *when* the cash arrives are equally important. Remember this thought when we cover the miracle of compounding savings later in **Chart 16.1**. View your family as a little business that also needs to look at free cash flow, timing of cash receipts, and increasing free cash flow over time. We will spend a lot of effort learning how to formulate and prepare a budget to plan for future bills.

We will endeavor, little by little, to keep increasing the inflow of money until it exceeds any current needs and the extra is diverted into investments that further help raise future cash flow (and net worth). The third leg of the stool is **careful and educated investment execution** (we'll cover that in upcoming chapters). Damn fine piece of furniture, that one.

BORROWING MONEY

The opposite of saving is borrowing. They are two poles of the same magnet, and any financial plan has to recognize that one tends to cancel out the other. Whenever you borrow money, you should sweat it. Money owed is an anchor around your neck, and you'd better be able to swim with it without drowning. Debt puts you directly into the control of another party. Sometimes debt is tolerable, as we shall discuss below. That lender may be a bank, your friend, or any one of a hundred other sources. As a person of financial integrity and sound money principles, you will always expect to repay what you have borrowed on the terms and conditions agreed upon when you took the lender's money.

There are at least four types of common borrowing, based on the reason for the loan, which most people encounter:

1. *Asset-oriented borrowing*: a loan to buy an asset or investment.
2. *Necessity borrowing*: a loan is to fund an extraordinary expense that is often unanticipated and unavoidable.
3. *Luxury borrowing*: discretionary borrowing to purchase something desired but perhaps not needed.
4. *Life-changing borrowing*: a loan for major phase changes in life. such as marriage, adoption, or retraining for a new profession.

When you borrow money, you create *leverage*. That term means that you are able to acquire or do something that, without the loan, would be beyond your means. Leverage can be positive or negative:

■ When what you buy becomes more valuable than the cost of the interest paid on the money, that is called *positive leverage*. You are using some borrowed funds to earn a profit and eventually repay the loan, with money left over for yourself.
■ However, there is a very dark side possibility: that the asset bought with borrowed funds can actually decrease in value. Then you still owe the money (the *principal*) and the interest, plus an additional loss in the gap between what the asset was worth when you bought it and what it is worth when you sell it. This is called *negative*

leverage, and it has financially ruined more people and companies than you can imagine.

In 2008, some of the biggest firms in the world, such as Lehman Brothers, Merrill Lynch, Bank of America, AIG, Citibank, Fannie Mae, Bear Stearns, and hundreds of others vanished or were severely harmed by **negative leverage**. They owned billions of dollars of assets purchased with borrowed funds, and the value of those assets plunged. At a more personal level, people who had invested in stocks, hedge funds, and other assets with borrowed money were likewise crushed by negative leverage when the value of their stocks and investments fell dramatically. Many of them lost everything when the repayment became due. That's no way to create wealth in America.

Common Borrowings:

1. BUYING AN APPRECIATING ASSET WITH EQUITY PLUS LEVERAGE

Let's return to our three types of loans and examine outcomes of borrowing. If we buy an asset such as a house that we expect to appreciate (it may not) but in which we have *meaningful equity*, everyone is very satisfied with the outcome of positive leverage in a rising home real estate market. No problems there. As prices appreciate, the amount of equity within the loan compared to the size of the loan increases. Thus the *loan-to-value ratio* (loan amount divided by the value of the home) is decreasing. A borrower can probably survive problems produced by later negative cyclical trends (falling prices) in area home values.

The borrowing to fund the part of the purchase price above the down payment (the mortgage **loan**) is a blend of discretionary and necessary expense, since you have to live somewhere and chose this home. It is the **equity** you put into the purchase that protects the lender and you from a possible negative downside.

HOME SWAPPING

FOR EXAMPLE, IF you buy a home for $250,000 and have a large equity down payment of $100,000 (40 percent of the home's cost), the mortgage loan you owe is $150,000. That translates into loan-to-value of 60 percent ($150,000/$250,000 = .60) on the property purchased. If there is a fall in the real estate market of 10 percent and you have to sell or move from the house, the decrease in value ($25,000) is well covered by your $100,000 of equity and makes it possible to repay your $150,000 mortgage and have $75,000 of cash left over. In the best of all worlds, you might have the income to continue with payments on the $150,000 mortgage or find a renter whose rental payment carries the house mortgage. You may then wish to wait for the market cycle to recover rather than sell the home in an unfavorable market and suffer the $25,000 loss.

But if you purchased the same home with an equity down payment of $12,500 (5 percent down), then you have a mortgage of $237,500 and a loan-to-value ratio of 95 percent ($237,500/$250,000 = .95). The same decline of 10 percent in the real estate market at the moment you must sell or move completely wipes out your equity down payment of $12,500 and leaves you $12,500 shy of enough cash from the sale to repay your mortgage. You will then have to make up the unfunded loss with other assets or future earnings, because the home was not worth as much as you had borrowed.

That was the problem hundreds of thousands of homeowners faced in the real estate meltdown of 2008. Buyers were lured to purchase homes largely because government agencies and other lenders were freely promoting such high-leverage home purchases with 5 percent and even 0 percent down payments (equity). Many unfortunate homeowners became trapped because they could not afford to sell their home in a collapsed market and had no hope of repaying the full amount of their mortgage obligation once they were unable to make their monthly payments. They had *negative equity* caused by negative leverage. Their home asset became an economic liability nightmare. Some workers who lost their jobs wanted to relocate to another area where more job opportunities existed. Unfortunately, they often ended up with unacceptable credit profiles that prevented buying or renting a new home in a better job market or even securing employment because of a poor credit history. Our PLAN, if followed carefully and combined with hard work and success, is designed to avoid this type of financial entrapment.

2. FUNDING AN EXTRAORDINARY EXPENSE WITH A LOAN

The second type of loan is thrust upon a borrower by circumstance and may not involve actively purchasing an asset. It is not discretionary. A good example is an unexpected health condition that runs up a huge hospital bill and/or curtails your income for an extended period. Such a major development can exceed your rainy-day fund.

Your ability to pay the interest and principal is largely dependent on your ongoing income stream plus your savings. A hospital is usually the lender in this type of loan and is more likely to work with a borrower to structure, and in some cases reduce, the loan according to your ability to pay. As long as you *service the debt* (make regular payments) or some good faith portion of it, you are likely to keep good credit and your head above water. In our **PLAN,** we will take several steps to be prepared for all but the most drastic of extraordinary lifetime expenses. For most people this strategy will prevent needing this type of loan.

3. PURCHASING A WASTING ASSET

This third type of borrowing can be the financial killer. It is purely discretionary. Examples of wasting assets are a new car that decreases in value the moment you drive it out of the showroom; an unfunded trip; a stereo system bought on credit; or an expensive luxury watch. When bad things happen and you cannot make payments on a wasting asset, you may or may not have other assets you can sell to repay what you owe. Don't expect a lot of sympathy here from the seller of the product or the lender. Everyone occasionally buys wasting assets to reward themselves or their family. It is perfectly acceptable to splurge on yourself and your family as long as you do not do it on credit.

4. LIFE-CHANGING PURCHASES

As you go through life, your decisions on when and how much money to borrow may undergo considerable change. A young couple just starting out may be able to put only a small down payment on a first home. If they have no dependents, then the risk of high leverage may be acceptable for some period of time. It depends on job security, prospects for salary advancement, and many other factors. But extra effort is necessary to consistently add to home equity and reduce the loan-to-value ratio as soon as possible. There are always the dangers inherent in cyclical markets and potential negative leverage. That reality may mean buying secondhand furniture and avoiding frivolous purchases (especially with additional borrowed funds).

Remember Commandment XV: The closer you come to owning outright what you buy and keep, the more financially sound your **PLAN** will become. Debt is a devil and its elimination removes a great source of friction and stress from everyone's life.

Loan officers at banks and other lenders have some general rules of the road for borrowers. Often the most common is calculating the ratio of monthly debt payments to your monthly income. This is called the *coverage ratio*. Simply put, it means that the income you have coming in is equal to or greater, by a certain percentage, than the outflows to service any borrowings. So if your monthly income is four times the amount of your monthly payments, the coverage ratio is 4:1. If your income is two times your monthly payment, the coverage ratio is 2:1. Here's another way to look at the same thing:

$$\frac{\textbf{Monthly Payments}}{\textbf{Monthly Income}} = \textbf{\% (Percent Score)}$$

The coverage ratio calculation and one banker's interpretation of it is presented in *Chart 6.2*.

– CHART 6.2 –
MONTHLY PAYMENTS AND INCOME

RATIO OF PAYMENTS TO INCOME	PERCEPTION OF MOST LENDERS	YOUR PLAN	COMMENT
< 25%	Great credit	OK	Solid start toward full control of wealth
25%-35%	Good ratio	Sometimes OK	Consider reducing
35%-45%	An acceptable limit on debt level	Active plan for debt reduction	Nearing financial trouble
> 45%	To be avoided except in unusual circumstances	Trouble zone	Possible for short period for first-time home buyer with rising income, or for extraordinary emergency

Our financial PLAN has as a primary goal the elimination of wasting asset borrowings and as much other debt as possible. The PLAN goes into place as soon as you enter the workforce and have an income. Even with large assets such as a home, you should do whatever is possible to earn income to repay mortgage debt more quickly than required by your lender. If it means taking a second job for a portion of your life or postponing some purchases for a while, so be it. Remember our commandment on working for reward, Commandment VI: Thou shalt not covet what thou art not willing to work for.

Apply income and profits from investing toward getting to the point where your family could pay off any borrowings (including a mortgage on your home) with liquid assets if needed. This goal makes you *safe and secure* no matter what comes along in life or cyclical financial markets. It is a great feeling when your financial life reaches and passes that threshold!

CREDIT CARDS ARE FOR CONVENIENCE ONLY

Credit cards are a curse and a blessing. This is such an important credit topic that I have singled it out for emphasis. Credit cards are excellent for purposes of monthly record-keeping and general convenience so you don't have to carry a significant amount of cash. The curse is the ease with which you may impulsively buy on credit, which can lead you to overspend on unneeded items. Think of credit lines like being in Las Vegas with lots of cash in your pocket—but choose to take in the shows and great food and ignore the lure of gambling.

It is critical to always know your monthly balance and pay it off in full when the statement arrives. A good way to assure this happens is to have the balance owed on all credit cards automatically deducted from your checking account every month. If you have a credit card balance you can't pay at the end of the month, your financial PLAN is per se inadequate. There is no debate here.

Commandment IX:
Thou shalt not carry a credit card balance as this
puts you in the devil's grasp.

Pay off your total balance monthly. If you can't bring yourself to do this, then cut up your credit cards and use a debit card or cash instead. This practice is fundamental to being safe and secure in your financial life.

CREDIT CARD BALANCES WILL TRAP YOU

TWO REASONS ARE justification for this strict rule in our financial PLAN:

FIRST, CREDIT CARD balances cost you some of the highest interest rates allowed by law. They are almost always at or near criminal levels: the annual rate can be upwards of 30 percent on certain cards. And if you miss a payment, the penalties and other charges can push costs up to 50 percent. Card issuers get away with these rates because the credit card industry argues they have greater risk due to debt unsecured by any collateral other than your name. Don't fall into this trap.

SECOND, MANY PITFALLS are hidden in the fine print of the credit card contract. And the fine print is constantly being changed to the advantage of the issuing company. Credit card companies tend to compute the interest rate they charge on unpaid balances monthly and not yearly. What does this mean to the borrower?

If you owe $1,000 on a card that states the unpaid balance rate is 18 percent, most people think that's $180 per year (0.18 x $1,000 = $180) on each $1,000 owed.

But since the card interest compounds monthly, the actual interest rate is 19.56 percent because of the interest the card company gets on each previous month's interest. The result is that your 18 percent interest rate costs $195.60 per year (0.1956 x $1,000 = $195.60) on each $1,000 owed.

There are lots of other buried problems with this type of loan. Even if you have a lot of free time to read and understand all the contracts, it's just a bad deal to carry a balance on a credit card. And you are being bad by ignoring one of the money commandments.

THE CREDIT SCORE EXAM

Your credit score is important to every facet of your financial plan. These scores are checked not only when you apply for a loan but also for a host of other purposes, such as applying for membership to a club, seeking a new job, or obtaining a credit card. We all need to monitor our credit reports from each of the three reporting bureaus for accuracy. The three agencies are **Equifax, TransUnion, and Experian**, all easily located on the Internet. You are entitled to one free credit report per year from each. To secure yours, just go online to their Web sites and get their address to request your credit report. You will have to furnish proof of who you are such as a copy of a driver's license, a utility bill, a passport, or other documentation. It is worth the time and effort. Once you have received the three reports, compare the information and judge it for accuracy.

Your **PLAN** is to always have an above-average credit score at every point in your life. Scores may range from 300 to 850 on a scale called FICO. You and your family can maintain a credit score in the 750-850 area with some simple planning. And that will aid you greatly in fulfilling our financial **PLAN**.

If you are turned down for credit and you think it's because of an error in your report, ask for changes and then request another report. Then track down the store or credit source, alert them to the mistake, and get it corrected. This is a painful but very necessary process.

How important is it to stay on top of your credit reports? Say you apply for a mortgage offered at 5 percent to someone with a good score. Due to an error your score is lower than it should be, and the lender prices the same loan at 8 or 9 percent (or even higher). That means tens of thousands of dollars of additional interest expense or thousands of dollars of refinancing costs until the mistake on the report is corrected.

BLACK BOX CREDIT SCORES

THERE IS SOME vagueness on how credit scores are calculated by the three bureaus. One strange thing is that if you never borrow money, you have a lower credit score. So every once in a while, buy something on credit and make monthly payments. Keep a reserve of cash that you would have used to make an outright buy. After a few months of making regular payments, pay off the balance owed. The interest you paid can be considered a cost of improving your credit score. The interest you earned on the funds you kept in your possession help offset the interest you paid.

We had each of our children take out a small loan when they first went to college and make a year of monthly payments. This established their creditworthiness as separate and distinct from ours. It worked very well.

There are some other basics to a healthy credit score. Don't open and then close charge accounts within a six-month period. As long as there is no annual fee, leave them open for years even if you have a zero balance. Keep a variety of credit accounts such as mortgages, revolving credit cards, lines of credit, and car leases.

When you are tempted to open a department-store account because you'll receive a onetime discount, remember that each time you apply for credit, it lowers your score. If the discount is negligible, don't apply.

7

HOW TO INVEST

There is no autopilot in your financial life. Any *safe and secure* investment that turns a profit and allows you to sleep soundly at night is a good choice. Over the years I have participated in and perhaps won or lost in most kinds of investing. The value of *The Money Plan* is my candid assessment of what has met those two criteria in my financial life. We are trying to adopt a defensive posture for making money while understanding that all profit comes from risk of one kind or another. Sometimes you will win and other times you will lose money. I just want you to have more items in the plus column.

There are professional investors who do things to make money that the normal family breadwinner cannot hope to do. Fine for them. I am not against any kind of normal investment in stocks, ETFs, bonds, real estate, or any other category. My allocation between these is just somewhat different than other people's.

■ ■ ■

DIVERSIFICATION
OF YOUR EGG BASKET

The single most important tool for *safety* in your financial basket, which is also most likely to get you to your long-term financial goals, is *diversification*. It means that you allocate your capital portfolio among choices that provide a variety of financial instruments, exposure to different industries, several degrees of liquidity, small and large assets, and a range of maturities by which your investments may return back to cash. Markets of all kinds run in cycles that are rarely predictable, so your overall portfolio should have segments that do well under the conditions in which another segment will lag behind or suffer. There are many factors that affect investment choices differently, including:

1. Interest rate changes
2. Home sales activity
3. Inflation
4. Political policies
5. Tax policies
6. Specific company issues
7. Wars
8. Catastrophic events
9. International happenings
10. A thousand other things

By diversifying you are doing a type of risk adjustment that fits in with our focus on safe and secure. There are three basic reasons many people don't diversify:

- They are too lazy to be proactive.
- They want to get rich quickly by chasing the latest high-flyer idea.

- They are uninformed about the importance of diversification.

None of these conditions should apply to you. Face the reality that you need a naturally defensive posture on the path of creating wealth in America. Tactics other than defensive are puerile and ineffectual.

So how can we easily grasp the concept of useful diversification and its importance? Let's suppose, for the sake of simplicity, that you live in a state that has only two companies in which you can invest. One makes snow shovels and the other one gardening tools. If you invest 100 percent of your money in Frosty's Snow Shovels, the stock may do very well in winter but stays even or declines in summer as demand for snow removal evaporates. On the other hand, if you invest 100 percent of your money in Green Garden Tools, the investment in its stock may be unexciting in winter when no one gardens but due for a healthy rise with profits in spring and summer months. What you really need is a steady investment return strategy to be in the correct companies on a year-round basis. The best solution might be to put half of your funds in each company so that, at any season in the year, other investors are excited about heightened seasonal profits for one company in your portfolio. (Remember that markets respond to the laws of supply and demand and a successful stock has more investors buying for strengthening top-line [sales] growth.) So in ·this illustration we have diversified into part of a year-round positive demand using our two companies.

Diversity needs to be everywhere in your financial life. It applies beyond money and its surrogates to institutions and knowledge. Here follows a partial plan for several kinds of diversity:

1. Divide your money among large financial institutions, so it is not all in the same place. Size really does matter if you

want these companies to be a buffer of protection for your assets. Check to see that they have excellent monthly reports, substantial assets, relatively low fees, and insurance beyond the government's basic coverage. (This will be important as you become more wealthy.) Don't be afraid to request an explanation of how you are protected in the worst-case scenario of an institutional failure. In 2008, that was not a far-fetched scenario when many banks and several well-known firms like Lehman Brothers and Merrill Lynch went broke.

2. Diversify your advisors as much as possible. (God created weather forecasters to make investment advisors look good.) Research the amount of money the advisor has under management, for how long he/she has worked, and ask for details on his/her education. Finally, check references. Pick few advisors who are young and in training; rather, select old and battle-scarred veterans. Listen well, but don't think any one of them should act without your full comprehension of what they are doing on your behalf. Remember, the word is "advisor," and you are the one calling the shots for an investment commitment. It's your money, not theirs.

3. Keep your records at home with a program like Quicken for your monthly updates, but also put a backup set in a safe-deposit box or Internet storage facility (such as www. carbonite.com) on a regular basis. Fires destroy computers and theft is always possible.

4. As your assets grow, place some of them in other family members' names. This is a simple and basic asset-protection step that diversifies money within your family. You would be amazed at how many people fail to take this important step.

5. Make sure your spouse has his/her own credit that is well established in their own name.

6. Diversify your financial reading. *The Wall Street Journal* is mandatory reading, although not every single page will be relevant. You can't get the whole picture from *The Wall Street Journal*, although it is better than any local paper in its reporting on financial news and the breadth of the markets. Second to it for daily input is the *Financial Times*. You may need the input of *Bloomberg Business Week*, *Forbes*, *Barron's*, *Kiplinger's Personal Finance*, and an investment letter or two. I particularly like Bob Brinker's *Marketimer* letter (www.bobbrinker.com) for his common sense. There are hundreds of market-related monthly publications. Morningstar has some interesting material you can preview at their Web site (www.Morningstar.com), as does Standard & Poor's (www.standardandpoors.com/). The world will not end if you don't read an issue immediately upon receipt, so forget about the "no time" excuse. The more you read the more you will become knowledgeable and able to form your own decisions for your **plan**.

Note a caveat here: don't go to an extreme with too much diversity. One ice-cream sundae tastes good. One chocolate sundae followed by an additional sundae from each of sixty-four flavors will upset your stomach. A good rule of thumb is to have about three institutions, including your bank, working for you. Mix a wide variety of categories within your universal portfolio. When it comes to individual stocks, most professionals agree that about twenty is the maximum number manageable. I prefer a number smaller than ten so that you can list them on a portfolio at www.yahoo.com and follow news developments within each company. Although I don't want you to own them exclusively, some mutual funds can make diversification easier because they are already diversified by definition (even if their broad focus is rather specific, i.e., global, small cap stocks, large cap stocks, dividends, and bonds, etc.). If you do decide on owning mutual funds, aim for five to eight of different types (we will discuss this later). Bonds in your portfolio should have a geographical diversification if they are municipal obligations, so exposure to any single state or project is not too heavily weighted. Likewise with corporate bonds or foreign sovereign bonds: the risk should be spread over industries and countries that have the best ratings.

At all of life's stages and in all circumstances, diversification is the safest investment path. Professional financiers call it "the only free lunch." The broader your diversification within acceptable investments, the larger your safety net. The overall portfolio can never return what your single best investment earned but, conversely, it will never fall as much as your worst selection. Everything in moderation and, to repeat that baseball analogy: try for many singles, a few doubles, and an occasional triple. Leave the temptation to swing for home runs to the professionals (who are likely to be using other people's money).

TAX IS A FOUR-LETTER WORD

The two kinds of tax that you will need to keep in mind for investing purposes are capital gains and ordinary income taxes. *Capital gains* taxes are assessed on the profit you realize from selling an investment such as a bond, stock, parcel of real estate, ETF, or mutual fund. The amount taxed is the difference between your *cost basis* (what you paid for the investment) and the *selling price* (the net amount you received when it was sold). That's your capital gain.

Capital gains taxes are also defined by the period of time you have held the asset. *Long-term capital gains* are currently defined as gains on an investment held for more than twelve months. *Short-term capital gains* are the gains on investments held for twelve months or less. This is important because long-term capital gains for individuals are currently taxed at a maximum rate of

15 percent while short-term capital gains are presently taxed at ordinary income-tax-bracket rates, which can go as high as 37.9 percent on earned income (including the 2.9 percent Medicare tax) and 35 percent on unearned income. Quite a difference in what you will keep for yourself! However, all these rates are likely to change as a plan unfolds to deal with the U.S. deficit.

Of course, you can also have capital losses on investments that you sell. Once again, there are *long-term capital losses* and *short-term capital losses* depending on the holding period. Net out your capital gains and losses (subtract losses from profits to get a net number to put on a tax return) each year to figure your required tax. Long-term investments and short-term transactions must be netted separately. Long- and short-term gains or losses are netted together to produce a final amount of gain or loss for the year.

Let's do an example:

- You sell two stocks that have been in your portfolio for more than a year. Company A has a gain of $500 and Company B has a loss of $200, producing a net long-term gain of $300 ($500 – $200 = $300).
- In the same year you sell two more stocks bought just a few months ago. Company C has a short-term capital gain of $100 and Company D has a short-term capital loss of $200, giving a net short-term capital loss of $100 ($100 – $200 = –$100).
- You arrive at a net number (the final or ultimate calculation)of $200 in capital gains by subtracting the $100 net short-term loss from the $300 net long-term gain ($300 – $100 = $200).
- The rate of tax you pay on the final gain is determined by whether it is long or short term and by your tax bracket. Obviously, long-term gains taxed no higher than15 percent are more favorable than short-term gains, which can be taxed at up to 39.6 percent.

The rules for a net loss are even more complex. Net short-term losses can only be used up to $3,000 per year against other kinds of ordinary income. Net short-term losses above this amount can be carried over into the following year. There are more rules but we will stop here. (If you are somewhat confused, then read on.)

In most cases, good tax preparers pay for themselves by picking up nuances of the tax code you are likely to miss. As I mentioned earlier, I use my CPA for both tax work and financial advice. It is a two-for-one relationship that makes me more important to him and conversely makes him more attentive to me. If you are just starting out and filing a basic 1040EZ tax form, you might prepare your return yourself and have a professional check it for accuracy. Once you do this chore, I bet that you will swear off losing a day or more of time, and some hair, in favor of paying a pro to get it done.

A tax-preparation program such as TurboTax is adequate for simpler returns, but if your investment portfolio is at all sophisticated, software may not be able to handle the complexity. It's simply not advisable to do your own taxes. If you are sick, you go to a doctor for his specialized training and the fact that he is up-to-date on the latest treatments. Likewise, the rules are always changing in federal and state tax laws. And the changes are coming along more rapidly every year as the government seeks to promote certain behaviors with tax breaks and punish others with additional tax burdens. The questions you might ask about a potential tax preparer are:

1. Educational background
2. Certification
3. Years in practice
4. Exactly who in the firm will do the work
5. Whether the tax preparer will stand by you in an audit for free or at a charge

6. Charges for each service
7. As always, references of actual customers

ALTERNATIVE MINIMUM TAX IS A GOTCHA

OUR TAX SYSTEM is supposed to be equitable, but the truth is that the alternative minimum tax is a shadow tax system that removes many of the benefits of what is supposed to be a normal, fair tax structure. The original idea for the alternative tax was to make sure the very rich paid their fair share even if they had certain tax shelters. However, since it was never indexed to inflation, the alternative minimum tax has ensnared many middle-class families never originally covered by the regulation. For this and another million reasons, the tax code is a mess.

One final word on the subject of taxes and their relationship to investing. It is always wise to minimize taxes you have to pay when structuring or selling an investment. But to do this you may need to hold an investment for a minimum *holding period* before you sell in order to qualify for long-term capital gains treatment (which is at a much lower rate). Sell too early and the gains will be taxed as ordinary income, in your highest tax bracket. However, each investment stands on its own and should be sold, *regardless of tax treatment*, if it is the right time to sell it. If you have invested wisely, you won't go broke paying taxes. Never allow the tax payment tail to wag the investment dog. If you own a stock and an event you anticipated happens as you predicted (introduction of a new product or a specific earnings level, etc.), and you have a large ordinary income gain, sell and be happy with your ordinary gain and paying the extra tax. If you decide other factors will lead you to keep the investment for the future capital gains holding period and it rises some more, so much the better. Let the changing investment circumstances themselves determine the timing of a sale and not the tax treatment. Many investors have seen their profits turn to losses because they held for too long in hopes of getting a more favorable tax treatment.

ECONOMIC ROLLERCOASTERS

The job of the Federal Reserve is to nudge the economy into the best possible posture to produce growth and stability. It is not an easy job as the financial system has a number of problems that need to be dealt with in very different ways. Pricing power and wage growth, interest rates, demand, and a host of other factors are specific results of a dynamic economy moving into different phases of the business cycle. Let's examine *inflation*, *deflation*, and *stagflation* and get an idea of how they can affect your investment decisions and overall portfolio.

▶ INFLATION

The Federal Reserve has the ability to print money and, in effect, create wealth up to a point. The newly printed money is a paper promise of dollar value that is widely accepted by people in exchange for goods and services. When too much money is put in circulation and the government exceeds its matching sources of tax revenue, the value of the currency decreases. Then we have *inflation*: a rise in the cost of borrowing followed by a rise in the general cost of living. Economists mostly agree that high rates of inflation are caused by excessive growth in the money supply. So creating new dollars is often how the economy enters a period of increased inflation.

Inflation is measured by the increase in the price index for goods and services, commonly referred to as the consumer price index (CPI). It is given as a percentage change in general price levels from some base period over time.

Inflation must be a factor in your PLAN calculations because it corrodes your purchasing power. It is a real cost, as we saw in our calculation of the future cost of sending a child to college, or retirement. Failure to consider the effects of inflation would leave you with insufficient funds to meet the actual tuition expenditure. One way of looking at inflation's effects is that the purchasing power of the money you earn decreases over time. Another way is to say the future expense grows. These are two expressions of the same thing.

The illusion of a wage increase is a good example of how inflation robs you of your wealth. In a time of 2 percent inflation, you may be given a 3 percent raise, about which you feel quite positive. You see the additional money in your paycheck and feel that you are making progress. However, what if in a time of zero inflation you are given a 1 percent raise and your take-home dollars are less than the amount of the 3 percent raise? Which is better? The answer is that these two alternatives are economically identical. In each case you gained 1 percent in purchasing power.

Mild inflation is probably good for the stock investor, as it is a sign the economy is growing. If you own stocks, you want the companies to be selling into a thriving economy and increasing their earnings.

But when inflation spikes, as it did in the 1970s (to 13 percent), that is very bad for financial assets. Companies face much higher borrowing costs as rates increase on their loans. Bond and CD holders are especially hard hit because they have contracted to a fixed income stream until maturity. Interest rate increases cause the value of debt securities (bonds) to decrease if they have a fixed rate lower than the current rates. Their purchasing power is reduced each year as they cannot achieve a "raise" of their investment income. In such a period, your bond portfolio does best if you have shorter maturities of bonds so that principal amounts are regularly coming due and can be reinvested in new bonds with higher coupon returns. (I'll go into more detail about this later in this chapter.)

There are several mutual funds and types of securities that are designed for investors who believe that inflation will become a major problem:

- The most direct investment is to buy Treasury Inflation-Protected Securities (*TIPS*), which are government bonds pegged to inflation using the CPI rate to calculate your return. TIPS are a sort of baseline insurance against a rise in the cost of living.
- The Vanguard Inflation-Protected Securities Fund, iShares Barclays TIPS Bond ETF, and Pimco Real Return Fund are good examples of inflation-resistant investments.

Finally, you may consider diversified commodity funds and precious metal investments such as SPDR Gold Trust ETF (symbol: GLD) and Fidelity Select Gold (symbol: FSAGX), iSHASRES Silver Trust (symbol: SLV), which invest in securities of companies whose principal business activity is in precious metals. These investments are not as risky as buying the commodity outright in coins or bars and do not present the problem of theft, storage, and redemption. You can locate these and other funds through your financial advisor or with a little time on the Internet. Do your homework if you want to hedge against inflation using this type of investment vehicle.

One type of investment that usually fares well in an inflationary period is real estate. Although higher interest rates do not make it easier to buy, inflation tends to push up prices, as buyers see tangible value in construction materials purchased in a prior period when they were less expensive. Guard against purchasing real estate at the top of the market and make sure you get good value in the right location. Your down-payment equity and cash flow should be substantial enough to carry the property under changing macroeconomic scenarios.

You should always be aware of the level of inflation and formulate a judgment as to how it will affect your future investment plans. It is one of the more important components of an investment strategy to consider in the overall portfolio.

▶ DEFLATION

The counterpart to inflation is *deflation*, which by some accounts is the more dangerous problem. Persistent declining prices produce a spiral of declining profits, unemployment, and a psychology that prevents the consumer from spending. In effect, the market has a strong supply of goods and a weakening demand for them. Mild deflation, like mild inflation, is not a worrisome macroeconomic problem. The damage comes from an expanding ripple effect when banks stop lending because they fear their collateral will decline as security; businesses stop expanding because demand for their products and services is weak; unemployment increases; and wages continue to fall.

Good strategies in a deflationary period include:

- Focusing on companies that have products considered a necessity for day-to-day living. Quality of stock and bond assets is a paramount concern during deflation.
- Increasing liquidity and having more near-cash investments.

Being very conservative is a central part of our PLAN in a deflationary period. If you see a sharp drop in the CPI, it is time to assume a defensive posture and wait for some indication the economy is turning around.

There have been some very long periods of deflation. For example, Japan entered one in the early 1990s that lasted the better part of two decades. In an effort to boost demand and investment, the Japanese government lowered interest rates to 0 percent, but still the economy failed to improve. It was not until July of 2006 that some inflation began to creep back and prices stabilized and began a healthy rise. We have had no such comparable length and severity of deflation in the United States and our many fiscal watchdogs make it unlikely. But it is always possible.

▶ STAGFLATION

Stagflation is persistent inflation and stagnant business activity happening at the same time, when prices for goods and services are surging at a time of slow economic growth. Generally, during stagflation, unemployment grows and consumers begin to act irrationally. Because people have come to expect continuous price increases, they stockpile in anticipation. The upward spiral of prices continues because there is greatly inflated demand.

We had this problem in the United States. in the 1970s under President Carter, when wages as well as huge government programs such as Social Security began to be pegged to a cost-of-living adjustment tied to the rising CPI. The government tried many strategies including voluntary wage control (ineffective), voluntary price guidelines (never happened), and getting out of certain heavily regulated industries such as telephone, trucking, and airlines. In addition, the Federal Reserve stopped supplying the money that inflation demanded. The result was an abrupt and deep recession in which consumers stopped spending and business ceased expanding.

It is very difficult to help insulate a portfolio against stagflation—there is no perfect hedge. Once again, the best focus is on high-quality bonds and solid stock-performance companies. Some gold, total return funds (funds that promise to deliver returns that beat the prevailing rate of interest and preserve capital at the same time), and TIPS will help to counter the risk on the inflation side if a large increase should come to pass. Liquidity, as always, is also prudent, as unsettled markets are likely to be quite volatile.

MEET AND GREET SOME NEW WORDS

We have covered some of the financial terminology that is useful for reading and properly understanding investment publications. I have tried to weed out the more esoteric concepts and vocabulary because our purpose is to develop a practical **PLAN** to build wealth, not to impress a business-school professor. If you want a more expansive grasp of terminology, sign up at www.InvestorWords.com for a free daily e-mail with a new word each day. Investor Words has an excellent financial glossary with some seventy-five hundred financial terms and is also a great gateway to about sixty thousand links to financial information. But in the meantime, let's add a few more concepts to our discussion.

▶ OPPORTUNITY COST

No investor can make every type of investment at once, because one of the more basic economic concepts is that resources are finite and opportunity is not. We have discussed how diversity is a key element of your PLAN, but you will still have to choose how to accomplish that diversity. Thus we have an *opportunity cost*, which is the value of the next-best investment alternative that you forgo as a result of a chosen investment. Opportunity cost assumes that both alternatives were desirable, but due to a scarcity of resources you could choose only one. So opportunity cost is a way of expressing the relationship between choice and resource limitations.

Consider college tuition. In the section on "Your Child Goes to College," we calculated that the cost of a four-year undergraduate degree might cost $142,000 for each child. This is an opportunity cost decision in the sense that:

1. Your child might have gone to work and earned an income instead of going to college.
2. You could have invested that money instead of spending it on tuition.
3. You could have paid off your home mortgage with those funds.
4. You could have purchased a new car or summer home, gone on a long vacation, or sprung for some other comfort.

The first three possibilities are economic-opportunity costs and the fourth demonstrates that opportunity cost is not restricted to financial considerations. Comfort and pleasure are also part of the equation.

Opportunity cost is not part of accounting, which does not consider or quantify effects produced by forgone opportunities. You won't see an opportunity-cost line on any financial statements; nor is it an exact calculation. But consider that when your PLAN directs your effort to pay off all debt, including your home mortgage, there is an implicit opportunity cost that you recognize for accomplishing that objective.

In the case of a home mortgage repaid, the borrowed funds *might* have been successfully invested to produce a return greater than the cost of the mortgage loan. However, as part of safe and secure, we accept that opportunity cost for the peace of mind in knowing that we cannot lose our home because of an inability to service a loan. In addition, we have the benefit of a significant reduction in the needed cash flow to remain living in the home. That is a big factor in deciding on how much money is necessary for retirement.

► RETURN ON INVESTMENT

The concept of *return on investment (ROI)* is an easy one to understand. It is a simple ratio of the net gain (or loss) on an investment divided by the amount of money invested. It can be a positive or a negative number. The most confusing part is that return on investment is also called *profit, rate of return, interest, profit/loss, simple ROI, gain/loss,* and *net income/loss.*

For example, if you invest $100,000 and receive back $125,000, the net profit is $25,000 and the return on investment is a positive 25 percent. If you invest $100,000 and receive back $90,000, the net loss is $10,000 and the return on investment is a negative 10 percent. The mathematical formula is:

$$\text{ROI} = \frac{\textbf{Gain (or loss) amount}}{\textbf{Investment cost}}$$

Many times you make this calculation before completing an investment in order to understand whether you have made progress or lost ground on that particular investment. So if you invest in the stock market at the top of a business cycle and stocks decline during a recession, you may decide to hold onto your stocks until the economic outlook improves (if you repeat your diligence and still like the companies you chose). But it is still useful to know where you stand today with respect to your initial investment.

In such a case, your ROI will be negative, giving you a percentage loss on paper. The stocks may or may not recover their lost ground in the future. Or they may break into a positive ROI in a strong business recovery. In stocks there is no certainty of profit, so you have a decision to make about holding on or selling out and taking your loss. Sometimes taking the loss is the wiser course of action if you have other profits to offset the loss for tax purposes. You might also have better investment uses for the remaining funds.

Note that in the case of bonds, the situation is a little different. When interest rates rise, the value of previously purchased bonds will decline if you have to sell them. The income available at the new interest rate is greater than the one on your old bonds. So *if you sell*, the investment will have a negative ROI. However, a quality bond held to maturity will return 100 percent of principal. If it was your intention to hold it to maturity, then interim business-cycle values are irrelevant.

Once again the Internet is full of ROI calculators that you can access for free. So all other things being equal—credit quality, maturity, liquidity, etc.—the investment with the higher ROI is the better investment. But it is just a formula, and as such will not account for risk.

▶ RETURN ON ASSETS

The *return on assets (ROA)* metric is usually used to determine how profitable a company is in relation to its peers. ROA tells you how many dollars of earnings management has derived from each dollar of assets it has under its control. When you invest in a stock or a bond, look for quality, earnings, and excellent ROA as important assurances of continued progress and stability. A company whose ROA is high compared to the competition's is probably well run, and your investment is likely to be secure.

Note in the formula below that ROA is an indicator of profitability before leverage (borrowings) is considered.

ROA = Net income + Interest expense – Interest tax savings / Total assets

The total value of the assets, arrived at after an evaluation by management, accountants, and other professionals, is stated on the **balance sheet** of every company. First satisfy yourself that the assets reflect reality and actual market value. If the company is audited by a large and reputable accounting firm, has a known law firm, has been in business a long time, has a good history of shareholder relations, and has respected management, it is likely to have reliable numbers. There are no guarantees, but it's as good as you can get. If you're not satisfied, look to invest elsewhere.

You will use ROA as one element in your financial analysis of investments. Once again, there is a wealth of information about it on the Internet. For example, if Company A has a net income of $4 million, with no borrowing, on assets of $20 million, its ROA is 20 percent. If Company B in the same industry has a net income of $2 million, with no borrowing, on the same assets of $20 million, its ROA is 10 percent. Based on this example, Company A does twice as good a job converting its assets into profit and is the better investment.

▶ MARKET CAP

This term does not refer to the top of a peanut butter jar. *Market cap*, or "market capitalization," is a way of categorizing companies by the amount of money investors feel the enterprise is worth.

Another way to look at it is as the net worth of a company. The basic formula is simple:

**Market cap = Number of shares outstanding
x share price**

If Company F has twelve million shares outstanding and each trades for $10 per share, the market cap is $120 million (12 x 10 = 120). The utility of a market cap is that it enables investors to categorize companies for comparison and risk. It would not be relevant to compare our Company F to Company G, which had a market cap of $120 billion, because the differential is far too great to be meaningful. Instead, there is general agreement on a scale of labels for various size categories. These are:

– CHART 7.1 –
MARKET CAPITALIZATION AND RISK

COMPANY CATEGORY	MARKET CAP	RISK OF INVESTMENT
Micro cap	Under $500 million (1)	Most risky
Small cap	$1 billion-$500 million	Risky but more stable
Mid cap	$10 billion - $1 billion	Good growth prospect
Large cap	$100 billion- $10 billion	Stable and international
Mega cap	Over $100 billion	Blue-chip quality

(1) Used to be $100 million but now grown to $500 million.

Within any market cap category, it is possible to gain some insight into how a company is being managed by comparing its growth, products, and yearly earnings to other similarly sized market cap companies within its industry. It's a good basis on which to invest the stock portion of your PLAN.

Smaller companies tend to grow faster (some at rates of 25 percent and more per year), and thus reward with very large returns those early investors who can tolerate the very large *risk premium*. (Reflect on the example of the profits of early investors in Microsoft, Google, and Facebook.) Small companies are very high risk, and fail at a much greater rate. Larger companies have a lower risk and often pay dividends as they grow. In the **PLAN**, I have favored high-dividend-paying stocks to increase our income/ cash flow. The larger company is a more safe and secure pick, if not as glamorous or potentially profitable. That is why it's called "investing" and not "winning." You must make choices between the risk associated with rapid growth versus more established dividend payers. It all goes back to your risk tolerance.

► PEG RATIO

In stocks the trick is to find a company whose earnings are growing much faster than the increase in its stock price. It is a good indication that the stock is undervalued and, at some point, its price will rise to reflect the correct P/E (price to earnings ratio). You'll make a profit.

But the reverse is also possible. Everyone may be jumping on board a stock and driving up its price to an unrealistic level, so that the first time the company slips just a little in its quarterly earnings report the stock price will tumble down. All quality brokers can furnish you with the *price to earnings to growth (PEG)* ratio on a given company, or you can look it up yourself at www. YahooFinance.com. If the PEG ratio is growing faster than the P/E ratio, avoid the stock as it likely will suffer a downdraft.

► EX-DIVIDEND DATE

The *ex-dividend date* is the day on which you must own a stock to qualify for receiving the dividend. Stock prices tend to rise in the period before this date since investors know they will receive a payment. Conversely, a stock will generally fall by the amount of its dividend when it begins to trade ex-dividend (after that date). The purchaser will have to wait for another period to receive another dividend payment.

The *record date* is established by the company to determine which *holders of record* are entitled to receive payment. You must be listed on the company's books on this date to receive a dividend. Stocks sell on three-day settlement for payment and transfer. So if you bought the stock on Wednesday and the record date is on Thursday, you won't receive a dividend because you're not yet listed on the company's books.

▶ CHARTING

Charting is a type of technical trading of stocks from graphs that give entry and exit points for a particular stock. It is not the same as trying to time the overall market or the state of the economy. Charting follows a specific company (or factor in the economy) that has shown a good correlation to price movement. However, it is based on historical data and there is no guarantee that what was true in the past will continue to be true in the future. Chartists contend that by graphing past history, an investor can find recurring trends that will generate a profit. For them there is no real understanding of the business itself but rather the observation of a mathematical pattern. Charting is a professional's game and more of a gamble than our PLAN usually allows.

Nevertheless, many charts on companies and averages are available online or from your broker, and these can provide helpful input on timing an investment. For example, if you are a fan of Microsoft and want to share in the company's future, a chart will tell you the high and low price in the last year and moving averages of prices, indicating better times to buy. The idea is to make your purchase below that highest point at some average level. This is also where *dollar cost averaging* can be applied (more on this concept in a few pages). If you select a few entry points and make several investments of a smaller amount at average entry prices, you may have a smaller total commitment and realize more profit than just buying all at once. For the stock portion of your PLAN, you likely will come to rely on certain charting measures as your comfort and skill with investing develops.

PRACTICE MAKES PERFECT (AGAIN)

THE INNOVATIVE, FREE, and relatively secure Web site www.Mint.com lets you set up an anonymous virtual investment account. Enter information about your bank, stocks, and credit cards; where you spend money; your debt; and a host of financial information. Mint.com has secure connections with more than seven thousand financial institutions. You'll receive weekly e-mails with your spending, investments, and any additional alerts you specify such as credit-card-bill due dates and low checking-account balance. The site claims that 90 percent of its users have altered their spending or savings patterns based on the information in the e-mails. It's a supplement to Quicken when you are pressed for time and want specific information.

1. MARKETS

RISK TOLERANCE

Since market movements are some part of the investment environment around our **PLAN** it is worthwhile at this point to have a brief discussion of how some people look at markets and how they invest in them. Investing is all about risk. That means that you anticipate a return on your investment but accept the potential that you can lose some or all of it. Your aim in your **PLAN** is to manage the risk and provide as much safety against catastrophic loss as possible. You want to hit a lot of singles and doubles on a regular basis, with an occasional home run and the inevitable strikeout. Approach each investment with an attitude of analysis, evaluation, and finally expectation of return in line with what the market offers for just keeping cash. Financial textbooks call this the *risk premium* or *risk-return tradeoff* in an investment. The textbooks define risk premium as the minimum difference a person requires to be willing to make an uncertain investment bet.

Many investors cannot tolerate the risk of market ups and downs. It's just not in their nature. They cannot relax when the business cycle turns negative or a financial crisis is reported time and again by the talking heads on twenty-four-hour news channels. Determine your *risk-tolerance level* and invest so you feel comfortable. You figure out your individual risk tolerance over time as you balance your successes and failures.

There are several sites online that can be helpful. Kiplinger's has a worksheet that accounts for some of the factors in risk tolerance and how their combination will influence your investment choices. The site www.kiplinger.com/tools/riskfind.html is worth a visit. If you want to read more on the subject check out "risk tolerance assessment," "risk tolerance level," or "risk tolerance calculator" at www.google.com.

That research may keep you from making expensive, knee-jerk decisions. In addition to personal handling of stress, your exposure to risk will change depending on your current stage in life. When you are young, with many more years of work ahead of you, it is acceptable to have a larger exposure to more volatile assets. If you lose money, there is still time to replace it. If you are about to retire, it is important to eliminate risk and preserve assets, because losses cannot so easily be replaced.

Risk premium is affected by many factors, starting at the moment of consideration and continuing until the investment is returned back into cash. Risk varies considerably with interest rates at the time of the investment and how they change during the term of the investment. It also varies with events in the local and national economy and the inflation rate. And risk premium is even influenced by what is happening in the world economy as a whole. This was quite evident in the 2008 meltdown, which severely affected all levels of investments throughout every economy in the world.

Here are a few risk premiums in the marketplace at the present point in time. Keep in mind that these are relative rates that constantly change with market interest rates and overall rates of inflation. Some of the relationships between each type of investment remain stable, but the world of money is always in flux. Our starting point is that cash is safest. After that we will define a money market fund that is invested in U.S. Treasury bills as a *risk-free return*, but in point of fact all investments have a slight risk of loss even if it is very unlikely to occur. On September 16, 2008, The Reserve Primary Fund in New York, a money market fund with $65 billion in assets, cut its share price (which had been, and as with any money market fund should always be, $1.00) to ninety-seven cents because of losses from IOUs it held from

Lehman Bros. Investors could not redeem their positions for up to seven days while this unprecedented event was unfolding. So all investments have some degree of risk associated with them. However, for all practical purposes we will consider money market funds by major companies to be risk-free. In 2009, rates on a money market fund were approximately 0.75 percent in a well-managed entity. Below, in **Chart 7.2**, are some associated risk premiums for several types of investments.

– **CHART 7.2** –
SAMPLE RISK PREMIUMS

INVESTMENT	RISK-FREE RETURN	RETURN EX-PECTATION	RISK PRE-MIUM ON IN-VESTMENT	COMMENT
Cash	0	0	0	
Money market	.75%	.75%	0	Almost the same as cash
CD	.75	.75	0	FDIC Insured
Bonds	.75%	2–8%	1.25–7.25%	Maturity, type, and credit of issuer are major factors
Individual stocks	.75%	8–20% +	7.25–19.25% +	Reflect volatility
Mutual funds	.75%	7–10%	6.25–9.25%	Diversification lowers risk
Real estate	.75%	8–50%	7.25–49.25%	Generally longer term
Hedge funds	.75%	30%	29.25%	
Commodities	.75%	20%	19.25%	
Start-up business	.75%	100%	99.25%	Risk lowered by your skill/ knowledge

The natural question to ask is, "What is the relationship between risk premium and our PLAN?" The answer is that we generally are not involved in the higher risk premium investments unless we have some direct knowledge or skill that significantly reduces the risk premium for us relative to other investors who seek these opportunities. Here are some examples:

- In a start-up software business, if we have special knowledge for writing a particular program solution that will be valuable to the marketplace, our risk premium is much lower than that of an ordinary investor.
- In the medical field, if we have the license and training to practice a particular procedure, then investing in a start-up using the license is much safer than relying on hired staff.
- If we know the real estate market very well in a particular area, we may be able to spot trends that a remote investor will miss.
- Lastly, if we are very familiar with an industry and its products, our stock picks may be better informed within that industry and thus carry a lower risk premium.

In the absence of a special advantage to lower your risk premium, play it safe. There is a long list of ways in which it is possible to lose money and only have a lesson to show for the effort. In general, these involve betting on the more esoteric investment vehicles that people commit to on an impulse or because they feel some kind of pressure to act "like the big boys." Sometimes the mistake happens after receiving a large sum of money from the sale of an asset, severance pay, an unusually large annual bonus, or an inheritance, when people see their investable asset base suddenly swell. (As Woody Allen said, "If only God would give me some clear sign. Like making a large deposit in my name at a Swiss bank.")

What should you do with such a windfall? Exercise great care. Don't let the money burn a hole in your pocket while you consider how to deploy the funds. People often have some feeling of urgency to do something immediately to make the recently received money begin working for their portfolio. You may be just as certain that poor choices can return the funds to strangers. What you avoid in your risk/reward analysis is just as important as what you choose.

BULLS, BEARS, AND SIMPLE ASSES

There are experts who believe the stock market has secular megatrends, which means a tendency to rise or fall over a longer period of time (five to ten years or more). Within the megatrends there are also cyclical trends (one to three years), which are shorter swings that can sometimes have large effects in value creation or destruction to a particular portfolio. The series of up-and-down cyclical trends happens as stocks correct for various economic events. The longer secular megatrends are what might interest us from the perspective of wealth building. Our **PLAN** involves obtaining wealth slowly and deliberately, as safely and securely as possible. We are making judgments on the future as we see it in fields such as electric autos, online shopping, scarcity of resources, aging of a population, actions of the government, advances in technology, etc. So let's spend a moment to go over a brief historical summary of past trends in stock markets. It might put us in good company with such marvelous megatrend investors as Warren Buffet and John Templeton.

NEW YORK STOCK EXCHANGE

THE NEW YORK Stock Exchange (NYSE) is considered the oldest and most prestigious place for a company to list. It has more than twenty-five hundred listings and it is from here that the Dow Jones Industrial average is measured. It is fully computerized and its quotes on stock prices are available almost instantly.

DOW JONES

THE *DOW JONES INDUSTRIAL AVERAGE* (DJIA), created in the nineteenth century, is the most watched stock market index. It is computed from the stock prices of thirty of the largest and most widely held public companies in the United States. Because it is price weighted to compensate for stock splits, it's not just an average of the prices of its components. This means that if a $20 stock increases in value by $3, it has the same effect as if a $40 stock increases in value by $3. Most investors consider the DJIA a proxy for the general stock market because its prestigious companies account for approximately 25 percent of the total market value. However, it does not include the smaller, quality companies that are also publicly traded and can be quite attractive to certain investors.

STANDARD & POORS

THE *STANDARD & POOR'S 500* (S&P500) is a second important index that includes five hundred of the leading companies in their industries, only some of which are very large. Since it contains approximately 70 percent of the total market value, some investors consider the S&P500 to be more representative of market direction. It is weighted by company size, so a price change of a large company has more influence than the same price change of a smaller company.

NASDAQ

THE ACRONYM NASDAQ stands for the National Association of Securities Dealer Automated Quotation system. It provides bid and asked quotes for about thirty-eight hundred companies that are not listed on other exchanges. Some very large companies, such as Microsoft, are listed there so it is incorrect to assume the NASDAQ is made up of only smaller entities. Aside from quotes, NASDAQ also provides regulatory and clearing functions for its companies. Symbols for NASDAQ companies are four letters long rather than the three-letter symbol from other exchanges.

Let's examine the roller-coaster ride of stocks through the past activity of the DJIA and the S&P500; you judge how it might fit in with your temperament and risk-tolerance level.

▶ A BRIEF LOOK AT BEAR MARKET DAMAGE IN STOCK MARKET HISTORY

When they are convinced that stock markets (or other types of markets such as commodities and bonds) are set to decline, *bear investors* sell shares they borrow from other investors in companies, in anticipation of buying shares more cheaply in the future and returning the borrowed shares to the investors. The *short seller* pays the share lender a set fee for using his shares. *Bull investors*, on the other hand, are convinced that there is going to be an economic boom and the price of shares in public companies (or the value of commodities, bonds, etc.) will rise to reflect the expanding underlying value. These investors believe they will be able to sell what they buy now at a profit in the future. Bears and bulls are each sometimes correct, and both methods should be respected. *Sheep investors*, however, are those who have no opinion and blindly rely on others for their financial decisions. Sheep investors are certain to be sheared to make nice coats for the bears and bulls.

In the last century, the longest secular bear market began on September 3, 1929, and continued until June 13, 1949. That twenty-year period saw the DJIA decline from 318.19 to 161.60, which translates to a whopping loss of 58 percent if we forget about dividends. Within that trend there were six cyclical bear trends and some pretty interesting cyclical bull trends that occurred until the bear megatrend finally ended in 1949. Then there began a major bull megatrend, which proved positive for investors for some fifteen years. Think about whether you would have had the patience to wait through such fluctuation and maintain confidence in your investment choices. It's very hard to do. That's why it is often said that a rising stock market must climb a wall of worry. For more information, see www.investopedia.com.

The next bear megatrend began on February 9, 1966, and finally bottomed on August 12, 1982, a period of sixteen years. During that time the DJIA declined 22 percent while the S&P500 gained only 0.5 percent annually excluding dividends. Then began a very rosy market period for the surviving stock investors, which continued (with the usual cyclical bear markets) to the end of the century.

On March 27, 2000, another secular bear megatrend began as measured by the DJIA and S&P500 indices. There have been several cyclical trends (two bear and two bull) so far within this ongoing bear megatrend. One of them demonstrates how stocks exhibit fairly extreme volatility that can panic investors into poor decisions. The DJIA closed at 14,164.53 on October 9, 2007, and then proceeded to decline to its March 9, 2009, low close of 6,547.05. That is a decline of approximately 54 percent during a period of seventeen months. The S&P500 had a similar fluctuation.

The largest one-day percentage drop in the DJIA occurred on Black Monday, October 19, 1987, when the average fell 22.61 percent in a single day (during a secular bull megatrend). To be fair, the largest one-day percentage gain occurred on March 15, 1933, when the DJIA rose 15.34 percent. (in the midst of a secular bear megatrend.) So stock investing within these changes is a volatility game that may fit our definition of safe and secure over long periods of time but generally is not our major focus. It is impossible to know where events will be at the moment you choose to exit the market.

►AVOIDING BULL MARKET DAMAGE

Bull market damage occurs when people who normally show a lot of common sense when purchasing a car or home lose their footing and jump into the market uninformed and vulnerable. They don't want to miss an opportunity and often buy at or near the peak of a cycle, then watch as their hard-earned money disappears when the cycle changes from bull to bear. What occurs next is even worse. It is encapsulated in the well-worn joke that a long-term investment is too often a short-term investment that failed. I believe that is largely true for inexperienced people. Many failed bull investors hang on to their previously irrational picks from the top of the market, hoping to break even by being patient over the years. It almost never happens. These investors become a different sort of animal—the stock market's simple asses.

Sometimes it does pay to hold a depressed stock for a long period in a changing market. Most often it pays to sell, take your loss and use it for tax purposes, and plan a new investment strategy. Judge each stock investment in your portfolio on the following basis: would you make it today, in the same dollar amount, under the current financial conditions? If the answer is no, then sell the investment and redeploy the assets. Every day is ground zero for a stock. Don't shy away from taking a loss when you have made a mistake by poorly timing the stock market bull, been wrong in your diligence, or received new information about the investment that changes your mind about its worthiness.

Remember Commandment VIII:
Thou shalt not swear at thy fate when things go badly
but roll up thy sleeves and get back to work.
(No one's listening anyway.)

Lastly, for heaven's sake don't double up to average down your cost on a stock unless you repeat your research and reaffirm your belief in the investment. Yesterday is not yours to recover, but today is your new chance to win with the correct strategy. Waiting for a second coming of a stock to prove that time fixes everything is an act of faith but not part of an investment *PLAN*.

FINANCIAL MARKETS ARE FOREVER BLOWING BUBBLES

What if two thousand people want to buy stocks? No problem. There are plenty of companies to go around and more than enough shares in the overall market. Then what happens if two million people want to buy stocks? Once again, no problem, but some of the later purchasers are likely to pay a higher price than the earlier buyers. The laws of supply and demand kick in. More people pushing on the demand side will provoke price increases in the total market because someone has to sell shares for someone to buy them. The sellers will recognize there is widespread demand for what they own and want a profit for the shares they surrender. Conversely, if there are many more sellers than buyers, lack of demand will force lower prices to encourage buyers to step in. That is how overall markets move up and down.

Now assume that all two million investors want to acquire their shares in Company XYZ on the same day. That is likely to cause a meteoric rise in share price as there is a huge imbalance between the normal number of willing daily sellers and the much larger number of eager buyers. This is a stock market bubble on the scale of a single company. At some point the price paid for a share in Company XYZ will no longer reflect the underlying corporate value but rather the buying frenzy. The last few purchasers are highly likely to suffer losses when the market returns to a normal level for Company XYZ because they invested in the company during a period of irrational exuberance.

The bubble principle can be seen in many different types of markets at various times. There is not always an easily identifiable cause. One explanation is that people sometimes have a herd mentality to do the same thing as others for fear of being left out. Greed is also a factor. These bubble periods are hard to resist because everyone wants to get on board the train before it leaves the station. At the height of the tulip mania in the fourteenth century, a prince traded his castle for two flowering bulbs. Before that bubble burst and tulips became widely available, it seems safe to say the bulb grower made a great profit from the hysteria of the crowd, and the prince acted foolishly to his great detriment.

You should avoid the onrushing train of hysterical people and get out of the station. Keep in mind that bubbles *always* burst and, if you are caught in the ensuing downdraft, the damage can be severe. In the financial meltdown of 2008, the resulting 40 percent slide in the stock market hurt most investors but allowed cheaper investment opportunity which helped many investors get back on their feet—but only after their family cars were repossessed to pay stock market losses. A lot of people suffered grave financial harm because they bought derivative financial instruments without understanding their underlying value or security. These folks acted rashly because everyone else seemed to be buying derivatives and making an easy profit. Following our **PLAN** we would have bought none of those instruments. Our **PLAN** is designed to steer you around the crowds into a slower, surer, and safer course.

We have had many real estate bubbles, technology bubbles (one burst in 2000), housing bubbles, hedge fund bubbles (one burst in 2008), commodity bubbles, private equity bubbles (the most recent in 2009), art bubbles, and precious metal bubbles. I will forever be amused by the former billionaire Nelson Bunker Hunt, who in the 1970s used his fortune to pump up a bubble in the silver market. Mr. Hunt and his group purchased 100 million ounces of silver starting from $11 an ounce all the way up to $50 an ounce. Their actions caused thousands of little investors to jump in, thus creating even more demand for the metal. When the silver bubble finally burst in 1980 and the price of an ounce of silver plunged back below $11, Mr. Hunt, once the world's richest man, ended up in Chapter 11. Leaving the courthouse he reportedly said, "A billion dollars is not what it used to be."

All markets have some natural cyclicality and there is easily available information on these trends at financial sites we have mentioned in previous chapters. Reading about repeatable trends should be part of your research before committing your hard-earned cash. But when things are rising rapidly, fanned by Internet and TV reporting that is designed to label it a phenomenon, watch out! There is a bubble on the horizon. Unless you want to lose value big time, avoid the bubbles and stick with the PLAN. The gust of wind from a bursting bubble can wallop your portfolio.

DOLLAR COST AVERAGING

All markets run in cycles that are not always predictable. People do not live forever, and as their needs change in their life cycle, so does their deployment of assets. Humans tend to travel through life in groups such as Baby Boomers (1946–1965), Generation X (1965–1980), Generation Y (1980–1995), and Generation Z (1995 onward). Their life changes are reflected in what they do with money, and these actions affect markets because large groups of individuals tend to act similarly.

Because the first part of our three-legged stool is a *safe and secure approach,* we want to minimize the impact of cyclicality as much as possible. Business cycles tend to swing up and down on a continuum of boom and bust. We can make this phenomenon work to our advantage by averaging out the swings in these cycles so that we do not invest all our funds at the peak of a cycle only to find ourselves falling steadily into its trough with a substantial loss of capital. Our goal is to invest a portion of our funds over time so we catch part of each stage of the business cycle. This is called *dollar cost averaging.*

No one can or should try to time the markets with all of their investable money in a single purchase. That technique is called *timing the market*. It's a fool's game and not part of our safe and secure PLAN. Investors who try to find the bottom, jump in with both feet, and attempt to sell at the top may win on occasion but will lose over time. Almost no one has done this successfully. www.Wikipedia.com and other sites have extensive material on why such predictive future market bets are dangerous. According to www.quickmba.com a market timer "must be correct 74 percent of the time to perform better than a passive portfolio of the same risk." Good luck!

There are thousands of professionals who have tried and failed get off the roller coaster at the correct moment. By using dollar cost averaging, you won't have to worry about where the markets are at any particular point in time. You will catch some of the highs and some of the lows, but in no case will your exposure be total. It works with stocks, bonds, mutual funds, some real estate, and in virtually every other investment category, including fine antiques and art.

The concept is to invest a relatively constant amount on a constant basis. There is no guessing about where the highs and lows are going to fall. Let's examine dollar cost averaging in an example from stock equity investing. You have $7,500 to invest in Company XYZ. You begin by purchasing one hundred shares using one-third of your funds. As the market cycles up and down, you decide to commit the rest of your capital in five $1,000 investments over time. That way all of your funds will not be entirely at risk on day one at a single price. *Chart 7.3* below shows how you would fare.

– CHART 7.3 –

DOLLAR COST AVERAGING MAKES SENSE

INVESTMENTS OVER TIME	PRICE/SHARE	TOTAL NUMBER OF SHARES	TOTAL INVESTMENT
1 (initial investment)	$25	100	$2,500
2	$27	37.04	$1,000
3	$22	45.45	$1,000
4	$20	50	$1,000
5	$22	45.45	$1,000
6	$26	38.46	$1,000
		316.4	$7,500

If you had invested all of your money at period one, your $7,500 would have purchased 300 shares with an average price of $25. By using dollar cost averaging, you were able to purchase 316.4 shares for the same money with an average cost per share of $23.70. You should also consider that, aside from getting the additional 16.4 shares for the same money investment, you increased your receipt of any dividend the stock might have paid during the periods. You also had control of part of your investment money during the periods between investments and earned some interest on it wherever it was held. You might also have happened on a better investment and can direct those funds there. Over a lifetime of an investment portfolio, dollar cost averaging gives a very meaningful boost to your assets as well as reducing your risk.

FINANCIAL HELPERS SOMETIMES DON'T

There are many kinds of consultants who offer financial planning services. My experience is that, while they may be helpful at times, no one knows your hopes and dreams better than you do.

And a financial **PLAN** is about achieving those objectives. It must be flexible enough to change when your life transitions unexpectedly. The surprise arrival of another child, a serious injury, a career shift, and a host of other unforeseen circumstances can, and probably will, occur. If you have a macro **PLAN**, these will only be bumps in the road and you will continue your life's journey nicely. However, at certain points you may want input from others.

Financial planners come in many shapes and sizes, with abilities following the same pattern. There are some professional designations that mean something, but even here you need to go for the gray hair that has experienced a few business cycles. These are some of the rungs on the ladder of training:

- *CFP*: This stands for Certified Financial Planner and is the highest designation in that category. At least these folks have some knowledge about investments, estate planning, retirement, and taxes. They have taken a few courses and qualified in an exam. They generally work for a fee and not for a commission. Does this make them more savvy than you? Not necessarily. Keep on top of things.
- **ChFC**: Chartered Financial Consultants have also completed some study and passed an exam. They must have at least three years of work experience in financial planning. Again, stay informed.
- **CPA** and **PFS**: To become a Certified Public Accountant is a big deal. The time and effort is significant, and there is no doubt that these professionals know their way around a company's balance sheet and income statement. The "PFS" says that they have taken specialized courses in financial planning. Does this necessarily translate into knowledge on investing? Sometimes. I have had a lot of success with this group, but it was

always based on looking carefully at their advice. I also tie in my tax work with my CPA, so there is a double incentive not to mess up.

- **CLU**: Charter Life Underwriters usually work for an insurance company and understand the products. They want to sell you something, but can be helpful if you look watchfully at their ideas. Be wary of fee-loaded policies.

- **BROKERS**: Stockbrokers don't have the word "broke" in their title for nothing. Brokers sell things and it is an unusual broker who is also a qualified advisor. A few are experienced professionals who can help you because they realize that, if they make you money, you will stay with them a long time. Many, however, just want to sell you the highest-commission deal possible and won't be around to pick up the pieces if it goes bust. If your stockbroker is not really knowledgeable about bonds as well as stocks, find a new one. The good ones are looking to manage larger accounts but may work with you if they see good earnings potential. Until you have some wealth it is easy to do stock purchases online yourself at the lowest cost possible. Bonds may require a broker, although Fidelity Investments and Charles Schwab, among others, cater to small bond buyers.

You can seek advice from a wide variety of people. But consider the management and investment of money to be your second job. In some ways, it is more important than your primary occupation. We will come back to this point many times in the following pages. Remember our fiscal mantra: "I am responsible for my financial dreams." The fact is—you are.

2. BONDS

WHY OUR PLAN EMPHASIZES MUNICIPAL BONDS

The municipal bond market has about 2.7 trillion dollars of securities, lots of bond purposes, tens of thousands of borrowers, a broad spectrum of credit choices, and is as close to a complete buffet table of income investments as any bond category. It has dozens of bond borrowing reasons such as water treatment, building schools, police stations, airports, roads, water works, jails, etc., and also stretches into activities such as student loans, retirement systems, and working capital for local government. So municipal bonds are highly diversified in their character as well as substance, and as we have discussed earlier, diversification is a good thing.

Sources of repayment for the borrowing are specifically defined for every municipal bond and you can examine each one before you buy it. That is another good thing. In many cases, the framework that defines the obligation of the borrower and the rights of the bondholder is written in a state constitution or statute, some local ordinance, the bond contract (laid out in the offering document), or a combination of two or more of such clearly written descriptions. These are very strong sources of comfort as they are backed by a broad-based taxing authority that can raise funds as needed. With stocks the return on your investment is dependent on the company doing well and the marketplace of other investors recognizing that fact and moving the price per share upwards.

The strength of the sources for returning your principal amount invested, and paying interest, determines the credit quality of a municipal bond. The stronger the enforceability language, and/or income stream supporting the legal obligation to repay, the higher the credit rating that will be assigned. With municipals an investor is not as dependent on vague market forces to achieve a profit on his investment as he would be if he invested in stocks. The expected profit is pretty well known at the time of purchase. You and your broker will still have to exercise some judgment to determine the actual capacity of the borrower if adverse circumstances like an economic meltdown happens along. For example, regardless of the assigned current credit rating of states like California, if deficit spending is a way of life as far as anyone can see into the future, it might be wise to choose a different borrower. Weak management practices in state, municipal, or local areas will always increase the vulnerability of your investment.

In our **PLAN**, we are acting safe and secure by purchasing municipal bonds that are above the minimum **investment-grade ratings** (at least BBB- or Baa3) and ignoring bonds below that level. Since 1970, municipal bonds in these categories have an extremely low default rate when compared to every other fixed income class. In fact, investment-grade municipal bonds as a group have a lower default rate than even "AAA" rated corporate bonds. Once again, that is a good thing. Standard & Poor's in 2009 released a municipal default study for the years 1986 through 2008 detailing how low the default rate really is for each municipal investment grade. For "A" rated municipal bonds during this period the overall default rate was only 0.11 percent compared with 3.34 percent for "A" rated U.S. corporate debt. The study also looked at borrowers in each year. For example in 1999, there were 2,208 municipal borrowers in the "AA" rated pool and ten years later only one had defaulted. That amounts to 0.05 percent of the pool. Perhaps we can change and add another certainty to an old expression, "The only things that are certain are death, taxes, and municipal investments." That's why a safe and secure money plan makes them a core investment holding.

Even if a municipal bond issue is in trouble it is quite likely that by the time things are dicey, the rating on the bond will have dropped many levels. You will have a chance to react and dispose of the investment to redeploy the funds elsewhere. Incidentally, the term "default" also includes instances where municipal bonds are not paying interest or principal in full and on time according to the terms of the initial obligation. In many cases, the borrower remedied the situation and made up the missed payment at a later date. Thus the purchasers of the bonds were made whole and no actual losses occurred. That is not often the case with corporate bonds where a default reflects a deteriorated business that is likely to enter bankruptcy court. It is also not common for stocks in failing smaller companies to reverse substantial share price drops.

THE NAME IS BONDS . . . MR. BONDS

In many ways bond investing is a unique methodology for slow wealth accumulation, but it does require some getting used to. You will have to work at mastering bonds in the same way that you study to become a doctor, lawyer, or engineer. No one else can do it for you, although you can get assistance. Bill Gates said it well when he was talking about all the advice he gets in his daily e-mail: "Like almost everyone who uses e-mail, I receive a ton of spam every day. Much of it offers to help me get out of debt or get rich quick. It would be funny if it weren't so exciting." Bill Gates did not become the richest man in the world by following get-rich-quick advice. He studied computers, thought a lot, devised his own plan, sought assistance with executing his plan, and then created Microsoft. No one else did it for him. It was his work product, just as your investment PLAN must be your own work product.

Bonds are a loan. They are a contract between you and some borrowing entity that has enough income to pay a set annual interest level (*coupon yield*) and then give you back your money (the *principal*) at a date certain in the future (*maturity*). As a class, bonds are a safer investment when compared to stocks, and I make them the core liquid asset of any of my portfolios. Stocks still have their place. But stocks can have negative years, while the income from a quality bond is quite predictable. If you want the miracle of compounding to work its hardest for you, then you want the fewest negative years because they dramatically affect the cumulative effect of a series of uninterrupted returns.

DIVIDEND-PAYING STOCKS

HIGH-QUALITY, DIVIDEND-PAYING STOCKS such as utilities and established companies with a history of increasing payout amounts can perform much like bonds in your investment portfolio. At some points in a stock market cycle these stocks have a yield comparable to bonds. According to Jeremy Siegel, a professor at the Wharton School of the University of Pennsylvania, if an investor had put $1,000 in a portfolio of the one hundred highest-yielding stocks in 1957, in 2009 the net accumulation would have been $450,000 (assuming the reinvestment of dividends). That is an annualized return of 12.5 percent, or 2.5 percent greater than the return on the S&P500 index.

There is more risk in these stocks at certain points in time than in a bond contract. Share price fluctuates, the dividend can be reduced, and stocks do not mature on a date certain. The dividend history of a stock and its yield at the time of purchase (dividend/share price = yield) can be found at finance.yahoo.com and in many other places on the Internet. There are also ETFs for dividend-paying stocks.

►BOND PERFORMANCE

The *coupon yield* of a bond pays you a yearly percentage income. Some professionals want to know the yield of a bond at the present moment, and this is called its *current yield* (current yield = annual payment/current price). You can pretty much ignore current yield as it does not provide a dynamic of the whole picture. You cannot compare bond investments based on their current yield because it does not reflect the market conditions that might change between purchase and maturity.

Another type of bond yield calculation tells you how much a bond will return over its lifetime: the *yield to maturity (YTM)*. This useful calculation does enable you to compare your bond investments. It assumes all coupon income and principal payment will be made and reinvested at the bond's promised yield at the time of the original investment. When you buy a bond, the **YTM** rate (and often the current yield) will be on the confirmation ticket, so you don't have to perform any calculations yourself. Yield to maturity can be thought of as the return on investment. It is always given as an annual percentage interest rate.

CALLABLE BONDS

A *CALLABLE BOND* is one in which the issuer has the right to pay the bond off prior to maturity under certain specified conditions. The issuer will explain at the time you purchase the bonds what those conditions are and when the right begins. Corporations often call their bonds in when the coupon interest on them is higher than prevailing market rates and they can pay off the old investors and reissue lower coupon bonds to new investors. This increases the company's cash flow by reducing the yearly bond interest and adding to the cash available for use in the business. Municipalities follow the same kind of thinking, so there are many callable municipal bonds as well. Obviously, an investor may be unhappy if his portfolio funds returned in the redemption can only be reinvested at a lower rate. Bonds are not usually called if rates have trended higher.

When bonds have a callable feature, they generally have a slightly better current yield at issuance because investors demand compensation for the risk of being paid off early and losing a higher income stream if rates have declined.

Don't assume that fixed-income bond or high-dividend-paying stock investing is for old folks—*nothing could be further from the truth*. Some investment advisors have unfairly maligned bonds and these special stocks as poor cousins of growth stocks. You can achieve capital appreciation in bond markets and dividend stocks that approaches the average returns on stock markets while being significantly more safe and secure. And you are likely to be more consistent in your returns, which means more miracle of compounding happiness. Even an exclusive bond portfolio of the highest quality (treasuries) can be designed to outperform stocks in certain markets. Over the last twenty years the S&P500 has returned only 7.7 percent annually, a full percentage point below the 8.7 percent return for treasury bonds with a maturity of ten or more years. In fact, long-term treasuries as measured by the Barclay's Capital Long Term Treasury Bond total return index have exceeded the one-,three-,five-,ten-,fifteen-, and twenty-year S&P 500 return as of mid-2010. In the meantime a portfolio of bonds enjoys an income flow and a bunch of tax advantages (especially with municipal bonds, which are basically tax-free income for federal and some state and local purposes).

Here is an example of an outstanding mutual fund that has subscribed to the fixed-income notion. Vanguard Wellington Fund (symbol: VWELX) was launched in 1929 and ranks in the top 5 percent of balanced mutual funds for five- and ten-year returns, according to Morningstar. A $10,000 investment made in 1929 and kept through the last eighty years of the Great Depression, World War II, the Cold War, Viet Nam, recessions, Iraq, and the current financial challenges, would be worth $4.8 million today. That is a record that any knowledgeable investor would like to have.

Throughout its history the Wellington Fund has maintained 30–40 percent of the portfolio in fixed-income investments and 60–70 percent in dividend-paying common stocks, and yet averaged an annualized return of 8 percent. Such a high rate of return demonstrates that fixed-income investments can build significant wealth safely and securely as a large part of our PLAN. It is also interesting to note that in the decade of 1967 through 1977, the Wellington Fund adopted a more aggressive approach and performed quite poorly. Once it returned to its more conservative roots, it again began to flourish.

▶ INTEREST RATES AND BOND PRICES

The first thing to understand about bonds is how the changes in market interest rates during a normal business cycle affect the value of bonds. In general, when interest rates increase, the value of previously issued bonds decreases. Conversely, when interest rates decline, the value of previously issued bonds increases.

Bonds are a stream of income that is fixed at the time of purchase. The common established monetary denomination for bond units is a $1,000 face value, although the actual price you pay for a bond may be greater or less than $1,000. The face value is referred to as *par value* when it is an even $1,000. Let's say you buy a $1,000 bond at par value that has a 5 percent interest rate (termed its *coupon rate*). That means that over a one-year period, your bond pays $50 (0.05 x $1,000 = $50) for each $1,000 bond unit you own until the bond matures and your $1,000 is returned. If you own ten of these bonds, then your income is $500 per year and you have invested $10,000. So far it's easy to understand.

- If a bond's coupon income is *less than* its yield to maturity, the bond is selling at a *discount*: You are buying a $1,000 bond for less than its face value of $1,000. The price of a bond depends on interest rates in the market at the time you are purchasing or selling it. Because market interest rates fluctuate, a discount means that rates rose after the bond was issued.

  Discount bond: YTM > Current yield > Coupon yield

- But if a bond's coupon rate is *greater* than its yield to maturity, then the bond is selling at a *premium*: you are buying a $1,000 bond for more than its face value of $1,000. This bond will still mature to pay only $1,000 of principal at the end of its life, so the amount above $1,000 that you pay will be lost. This usually means that interest rates dropped after the bond was issued and resold to you.

  Premium bond: Coupon yield > Current yield > YTM

- Lastly, if a bond's coupon rate is equal to its yield to maturity, then the bond is selling at *par*: you are buying a $1,000 bond for its face value of $1,000. It is likely a new issue and has not yet been affected by any interest rate changes. It can also mean that rates are currently the same as when the bond was first issued.

Par bond: YTM = Current yield = Coupon yield

DOLLARS VERSUS BASIS POINTS

STOCKS ARE TRADED in *dollar increments*, so that a stock selling for 21 5/8 means that the price is 21 dollars and .625 cents (compute the 5/8 fraction to $.625). Since there are 100 cents in a dollar, in stocks 1/8 is .125 cents, 1/4 is .25 cents, 1/2 is .50 cents.

Bonds are also traded in increments of 100, but the number refers to fractions of a percentage point. A *basis point* is a unit equal to 1/100th of 1 percent and that is how bonds are commonly priced. So a bond whose yield increases from 4 percent to 4.5 percent is said to have its yield increased by 50 basis points, meaning its yield has increased by half a percentage point. A bond whose rate changes from 3 percent to 4 percent reflects a change of 1 percent, or 100 basis points.

Let's review this again. Assume that the bond market interest rates drop from 5 to 4 percent because the economy is slowing and many more people want to exit other investment vehicles (stocks, mutual funds, etc.) and buy the safer and certain income associated with bonds. More money available for bond issuers means that bond issuers can pay less to borrow. Ergo, they offer only 4 percent coupon rates on new $1,000 bonds and people still buy them. That means that the *income stream* from each new

$1,000 bond has fallen from $50 to $40 per year. The *cash flow* on $10,000 at the lower rate would be $400 (0.04 x $10,000 = $400).

But the bonds previously bought at a 5 percent rate still pay $50 per year until they mature, so someone who is buying new bonds at a 4 percent coupon might be willing to pay us a *premium* of, say, $20 per bond (total value for each bond is $20 + $1,000= $1,020). That buyer would get the additional $10 per year income from each of your older bonds issued when rates were higher. If you decide to sell your ten 5 percent bonds, you would receive $10,200 on your $10,000 investment (10 x $1020 = $10,200).

Plus you receive all the 5 percent income up to the day you sell the bond (called *accrued interest*). In an additional benefit, that $200 premium you receive on the sale of your older bonds (owned for the required time period) is a capital gain for tax purposes, not ordinary income, as the interest is on most bonds except municipal bonds. Remember, capital gains are taxed at a lower rate than ordinary income, so you keep more of your profit.

Now let's look at the other side of this basic bond concept. You purchased a par value $1,000 bond when rates were 4 percent, but the economy has heated up and there is a huge demand for borrowed money. Bond issuers are now willing to pay 5 percent to borrow the same $1,000 of par value. You are getting $40 per year income from each of your bonds, but new bonds would provide $50 per year. You have two choices:

1. You can hold your 4 percent bond until maturity while collecting $40 each year and get back your full $1,000 face value at maturity.
2. You can sell your bond at a *discount* of, say, $20 per bond ($1,000 – $20 = $980) and reinvest the proceeds in new 5 percent bonds to increase your cash flow.

If you decide to sell your ten 4 percent bonds, you would receive $9,800 on your $10,000 investment (10 x $980 = $9,800). That means that you had an actual loss of $200. However, depending on maturity date of the new bond, the increased cash flow ($50 versus $40 per year) would make you whole if it was a twenty-year bond. In addition, you can use this $200 capital loss to offset other capital gains on your tax return. It is no different than buying a stock for $10,000 and selling it for $9,800 when it declines in value and you decide on purchasing a different stock. Let's do a little review:

- *Why would someone pay a bond premium?* Perhaps they desire a higher cash flow and are not as concerned with the additional amount of money they have to pay as a premium to get it.
- *When the bond matures, what happens to that $20 premium?* The matured bond will only pay the $1,000 face value. The $20 premium was received a little each year in the form of increased cash flow (5 percent versus the market rate of 4 percent). The investor got the $200 premium back over time in better cash flow, so there was no actual loss at maturity. With premium bonds there is no capital loss to use as a deduction for tax purposes.

When interest rates change, you can have either losses or gains on bonds, just like stocks. The difference is that bonds have a fixed income set on the date of purchase/issue. If held to maturity, they will return only your $1,000 face value.

BONDS GET A REPORT CARD
LIKE YOUR KIDS

Bond credit ratings assess the creditworthiness of the issuer of a bond. Just like with your kid's report cards, we like to see a lot of "As" to fit in with our safe and secure philosophy. A small percentage of speculative "BBBs" is sometimes acceptable, but the "C" and "D" ratings are not included in our PLAN. Credit ratings give some indication of the potential for default on a bond. It's not that different from passing your own credit test.

The bond market is comprised of many issuers, from start-up companies (every bit as speculative as high-flying penny stocks) to ultra-safe government treasury entities. The higher the risk rating assigned to a bond, the higher the coupon rate will be and the higher the likelihood that you might never see the return of your principal amount when the bond matures. In our PLAN, we are seeking safety and security with reliable income stability. The choices of bonds that you should consider for your portfolios are listed here by bond type, starting from the safest treasuries and continuing on in increasing risk profile:

1. *U.S. government:* Treasuries have no chance for default and are at the top of the quality pile. By and large these are taxable instruments. The lower coupon rate (when compared to corporate bonds or municipal bonds) reflects their security, and so they pay the least after-tax returns. They represent the gold standard for safety but may be beyond the level of security you need because they provide a lower income stream. We are attempting to strike a balance in our PLAN between security and income. However, there is a place for treasuries for older investors and for those whose portfolio is large enough

that the reduced income will not affect lifestyle. The U.S. government smorgasbord of treasury bonds includes:

a. *Treasury bills:* These are sold at maturities from a few days to up to one year. No interest is paid prior to maturity as these bonds are sold at an original issue discount and mature at par. They are highly liquid, very safe, lower return, and a good place to park money for a short period.

b. *Treasury notes:* These notes mature in two to ten years and have a coupon payment every six months. T-notes are quoted in the secondary market in thirty-seconds of a point and are very liquid. Denominations run from $100 to $1,000,000. You may buy them direct from the U.S. Treasury (www. USTreasury.com) or in the secondary market.

c. *Treasury bonds:* T-bonds have the longest maturity, ranging from twenty to thirty years with a twice-yearly coupon payment. Once again they are highly liquid and safe, but you do give up yield for those attributes. T-bonds are more useful for long-term wish-list items for which you require the highest certainty. T-bonds are also useful for seniors no longer in the workforce who cannot afford to lose any of their retirement money. As with any fixed income investment, keep in mind that inflation eats away at the return over time.

d. *I savings bonds (TIPS):* These bonds are sold at face value from financial firms or directly from the U.S. Treasury, in denominations up to $10,000 in maturities up to thirty years. They are exempt from state and local taxes. If used to fund college expenses, the interest is exempt from federal taxes as well. I-bonds have a two-section interest rate. The first part is fixed at purchase and the second part is variable, tied to the Consumer Price Index. The total rate is adjusted twice each year. Go to www.savingsbonds.com for all the information you could need on these bonds.

e. *Savings bonds:* These bonds are called "Series EE" and "Series HH" bonds by Uncle Sam, and are sold at large discounts to face. They are often for sale at your local bank. (A large discount means you pay less than par when you buy them. So a $100 bond may only cost $70 but look like a $100 wedding gift!) They are mostly useful as gifts. Since they are nonmarketable and illiquid, they are not part of our investment **PLAN**.

2. *U.S. Agency Bonds:* Close to the gold standard of treasury securities, these bonds have a slightly lower level of government backing. U.S. agency bonds come with what is referred to as an "indirect government guarantee" and are unlikely to default, but can do so legally. They are issued by a series of federal organizations including Fannie Mae, Freddie Mac, Ginnie Mae, and Sallie Mae. The yield is only slightly higher than a treasury bond. They are fixed-rate debt securities with fixed maturities.

3. *Build America Bonds:* As part of the American Recovery and Reinvestment Act of 2009, this category of federal subsidy payment bond was established to lower borrowing costs for state and local governments. These bonds are taxable at a federal level and are best compared to corporate bonds rather than tax-free municipal bonds. They have a federal subsidy of 35 percent of the interest cost to the issuer—that is, the bondholder gets a federal tax credit of 35 percent of the interest income. However, the feds do not guarantee any principal or interest. Since

they are taxable, they are suitable for holding in an IRA in the same way as a corporate bond.

4. *Municipal bonds:* Municipals are offered by states, cities, and local governments. They can be backed by the general taxing authority or by a specific revenue stream from a project. The funds raised by the bond issue are used to finance a highway, hospital, or utility. Municipals are exempt from federal income tax and, in many cases, from state taxes. Because municipal bond income is tax free, we need to calculate a *taxable equivalent yield* when comparing municipal bonds to taxable corporate or government bonds. (More about this later.)

5. *Investment-grade corporate bonds:* Corporate bonds depend on the strength of the issuing company. The risk of default is generally higher than for municipal bonds, but still quite low. All coupon income is taxable like any other interest in the year it is received.

6. *Foreign bonds:* Bonds issued by foreign governments or large overseas companies often carry an additional risk of currency fluctuations. However, some are quite high quality and can be part of our PLAN. For example, when the dollar is likely to sink in relative value, you might purchase Canadian government bonds for diversification in your universal portfolio, thus protecting some portion of your assets from the reduced purchasing power of a slipping dollar. The Canadian bonds would increase in value if the currency of Canada gained strength against the dollar. All income is taxable in the year in which it is received.

7. *What we do not buy:*
    a. *Junk bonds:* These are below investment grade and come with a high risk. Why do you think they call them "junk"?

b. *Unrated bonds:* Go to Las Vegas and gamble there, not in your bond portfolio. These are unrated because no one can assess their risk. That's not part of our safe and secure PLAN.

BOND RATINGS

ALL U.S. GOVERNMENT bonds get the gold standard of AAA, and all other bonds are given ratings by professional analysts. There are two companies that rate bonds: Moody's (www.Moodys.com) and Standard & Poor's (www.standardandpoors.com). We are interested only in *investment-grade* bonds for our portfolio. Those are bonds that are relatively safe and have a rating above **Baa2** in the Moody's scale or above BBB on the Standard and Poor's scale. Your broker or the rating agency Web sites will furnish the rating on a potential investment.

Structure your bond portfolio as follows:

- **MOST BONDS SHOULD** fall in the middle ratings: Moody's **A1** to **A3**; S&P's **A+** to **A-**.
- **SOME IN THE** highest rating: Moody's **AAA** to **AA3**; S&P's **AAA** to **AA**.
- **ONLY A FEW** in the lower investment-grade category: Moody's **BAA1** to **BAA3**; S&P's **BBB+** to **BBB-**.

▶ ZERO-COUPON BONDS

All of the bond types we discussed above are differentiated by the issuer of the loan being willing to pay an annual, regular income as part of the bond contract. *Zero-coupon bonds* ("*zeros*") are a variation on traditional coupon bonds and occupy a category all by themselves. As the name implies, the bond has a 0 percent coupon and pays no regular yearly income from issuance to its maturity. The face value is still $1,000, but it is sold at a deep discount to its face value and *accretes* (increases in value) to par when it is finally paid off. For example, you might purchase a fifteen-year zero-coupon bond for forty cents of value on each dollar of full-face value at maturity. That means you pay $400 now for each $1,000 bond but expect no yearly income until it matures at face value. In effect, you receive all of your accumulated interest in one lump sum when you collect $1,000 at maturity for a $400 investment. Most of the issuers of zeros choose this type of bond because they do not have the yearly obligation to use up cash to pay semiyearly coupon interest.

Zero-coupon bonds are one of the cornerstones of our investment portfolio.

They are very useful to provide a certain sum of money needed at a future date. So a zero-coupon bond is ideal for far-off college expenses, planning a wedding, saving for a new home, or many other large-ticket items. We shall cover their use in further sections of our **PLAN**. Zero-coupon bonds have the following unique characteristics:

- There is no *reinvestment risk* with a zero-coupon bond. When you receive interest on other types of bonds, the money you receive may not be able to earn the same rate of return that was available at the time the original bond was issued. If, for example, the original rate drops from 5 percent coupons to a market rate of 4 percent coupons, the lower interest reduces available market cash flow considerably: you will be receiving $40 instead of

$50 per $1,000 bond and that is a 20 percent reduction on your reinvested coupon income. You can only reinvest the income you receive from a traditional bond each time it is received at the then-current, and often lower, rate. This reinvestment risk hurts your income stream and becomes more significant the longer it continues. Of course the reverse is true if rates rise from 5 percent coupons to 6 percent coupons and in that situation your income stream would improve.

Since a zero-coupon bond accretes by accumulating income until it grows to $1,000 of par value, it actually pays interest-on-interest upon your yearly accretion at the same rate of interest at which you purchased the bond. You earn the same rate of return on the money you invested *plus* the yearly accretion. Zeros are affected by changes in interest rates if you have to sell them prior to maturity, but if you keep them until the end you can count on a constant return from issuance to maturity. That is very important for planning purposes.

■ Each year you will pay federal taxes on the accretion amount earned in your zero-coupon bonds even though you receive no actual cash. So you need other income to pay the taxes each year on the accreted portion. At maturity you have no tax on the $1,000 received for each matured bond. However, if you are holding *tax-free municipal zeros*, you will pay no tax yearly *or* at maturity. Here is a great vehicle for long-range financial planning, which we will use extensively in our later discussions.

■ Zero-coupon bonds (and many of the other types) are sometimes called before they mature. This means that the issuer is redeeming them early and paying a set amount of money for each $1,000 of face value. A *right to early redemption* is revealed to the buyer at the time of purchase. It's not always a bad thing because often there is some additional payment benefit (premium for redemption) to giving up your bond early. Why would an issuer redeem its bonds? Usually it is because rates have declined and the issuer can sell new bonds with a lower interest rate.

BOND LADDERS YOU CAN STAND ON

A *bond ladder* is a strategy for building a bond portfolio of municipals, treasuries, and CDs that allows you to create dependable income and still have some measure of insulation from the market fluctuation in yield-curve interest rates. The bond ladder staggers bond maturities over time so that there is an even flow in the receipt of principal for *reinvestment* within a portfolio. As time goes on, each year (or whatever interval is chosen) the portfolio has the ability to reinvest at the current interest rates. Remember, when a bond matures, you cannot predict if interest rates will be higher, lower, or the same as the moment when you purchased the bond.

There is always the risk that, if rates are lower now than when you first purchased a bond, your yearly reinvested income or principal will earn a reduced rate compared to what was obtainable in the past. Conversely, if available market rates have increased, you would want some part of the portfolio to mature so that you can reinvest and take advantage of the prevailing higher rates. Either way, you don't want to be totally locked in to a single maturity for all your funds. Since there are always fluctuations in the yield curve, some of your investable funds should become available before the latest maturity date in your ladder. That will provide needed flexibility in your portfolio for liquidity.

A bond ladder is just another form of diversification in which you have some portion of bonds, treasuries,or CDs mature in staggered fashion: two, four, six, ten, twelve, fifteen years, etc. Notice that this bond ladder does not need to have rungs in every single year. What you want from a ladder is:

1. Dependable income for the period of time you choose.
2. Some liquidity generated along the way.
3. A lowered risk compared to having a single date determine your bond income.
4. A mix of issuers.
5. Some mix of bond types (such as municipal and corporate).

If you have less than $25,000 to invest, then a bond mutual fund may be an acceptable way to stagger maturity dates because the pooled money will enable the manager to create a diversified ladder. However, if interest rates are rising, the **value of shares** in a bond mutual fund will fall and you will lose part of your principal if you sell. The price of the mutual fund bond shares is NOT in your control; there is no finite maturity date that returns all of what you invested. The same is not true for bonds, treasuries, and CDs you own outright and that you can hold until maturity and receive a return of the full principal amount. Our selection of a $25,000 amount is not a hard-and-fast rule—if your income is somewhat secure (engineer, lawyer, doctor, computer specialist, etc.), then you can begin your PLAN by buying individual bonds and keep filling in the ladder each time additional investment funds become available. This method lets you construct the rungs of your ladder over time but slightly increases your risk because not as many dates have maturing bonds to provide liquidity. It's also more work for you, but the payoff of owning bonds outright is better control over your investments. An ideal base level bond ladder has an investable portfolio of $500,000–$1 million. Of course, there is no upper limit.

YIELD CURVES ARE NOT PART OF BASEBALL

WHEN INVESTING IN bonds the yield curve is the relationship between the interest rate and the time to maturity of the debt. It is what the borrower has to pay the lender (you) to get them to part with their money for a period of time. The longer the period of time, the greater the interest rate in most cases. The yield curve is also affected by many factors such as creditworthiness, liquidity, and market perception. Yield curves are commonly plotted out as a graph and many Web sites have them. If you want to learn more, go to www.google.com and plug in the term.

Before you buy a bond for your ladder, it is a good idea to track the price where the bond has traded. A free Web site that posts trades for your comparison is www.investigatingbonds.com. There are also brokers such as E*Trade, Charles Schwab, and Bond-desk to check that you are getting a good deal on your purchase. In general, you can expect to pay ¾ to 2 percentage points commission over the price. Sales commissions do vary widely depending on the size of your portfolio and the size of the purchase you are making (often referred to as the "**block**"). However, consider that by comparison Pimco Total Return fund (PTTAX) has a 3.5 percent **load** (the commission paid to buy it) and a yearly cost of 0.90 percent in its expense ratio.

There is a minimum period of six to seven years for a bond ladder to have any demonstrable benefit, but the final maturity can match almost any length of time to meet your liquidity and cash flow needs. The more rungs you have in a bond ladder, the more diversified and flexible it is. Your goal is gradually to get to the point that you have some investment funds come due each year. When you do reach that point, if you reinvest some or all income with maturing principal each year, it is almost the same as dollar-cost averaging of stocks. The main difference is that you are smoothing out the effects of fluctuations in available market yields. You can calculate income from a bond ladder for most any mix of bonds, CDs, income ETFs, and treasury issues with an Income Ladder Calculator at www.incomeladders.com.

SOME FINAL BOND CONCEPTS

There is an advantage in the value of an income stream of a financial instrument when the higher yield lasts for a longer time during a period of relatively stable interest rates. A five-year bond that pays a coupon of 4 percent will return five years of income at $40 per $1,000 bond. A ten-year bond that pays 4 percent will produce the same income, but for twice as long. If an investor's time frame is ten years of income, then the certainty of the ten-year income stream is better than the risk of having to search in five years for a new bond paying 4 percent. That is commonly referred to as *locking in a yield*. Of course, the disadvantage is if rates rise and you are locked into a lower rate. It's all part of risk management and how you decide to develop your PLAN.

Basis point value measures interest rate risk over time as yield curves change with credit market fluctuations. Basis point value tells you how much money your bonds will gain or lose for 0.01 percent (one basis point) of movement in the yield curve. It is a method to quantify an interest-rate risk for the changes in market yield interest rates. Remember *present value* and *future value*? If we want to properly value a bond at this present moment, we need to discount its income stream to price it at what the market will bear today. We are finding the present value of our bonds when we *mark to market* at existing yield curve conditions. We'll do this now as an instructional exercise, but as a practical matter your broker will furnish these numbers. However, it is important to understand that *the longer the time to a bond's maturity date, the more interest rate movements affect its value.*

We are going to use large numbers in our example to highlight the changes, but the principle applies in the same manner for smaller amounts of bonds as well as larger positions:

- You buy one hundred five-year bonds at par with a 5 per-cent coupon at par. Your total investment is $100,000:

    100 bonds x $1,000 per bond = $100,000

- If interest rates move up to 5.01 percent (a change of one basis point), then the current market value of the bond changes for a one-basis-point move in the market yields a negative amount so the bond is worth slightly less IF IT WERE TO BE SOLD. If the bond is not sold but is being held to maturity, the interest rate change is meaningless because it pays according to the original terms at the time of purchase.

- How do you find this value change? Go to the Internet and choose a *bond value calculator.* AOL Money & Finance has a good one at www.money.aol.com/calcu-lators/bonds. Select "How will rate changes affect my bond's current value?" Plug in the price you paid as a percentage of face value (100 percent since you bought at par), time to maturity in years (5), coupon interest rate (5 percent), and market interest rate/year (5.01 percent) and press the calculate bond value button. The current bond value is computed at $99,756 if inter-est rates stay at 5.01 percent. The difference is a loss in value of $244 if you sell the bond today.

- The calculator also tells us automatically, for comparison, that if yield curve interest rates had moved down 2 full percentage points (200 basis points), you would have gained $9,093 in a sale. If yield curve interest rates had moved up 2 full percentage points, you would have lost $8,708 if you sold the bond.

Now let's take our example one step further. What if it was a twenty-year bond and everything else were the same? The only plug-in you change is the time to maturity, which is now twenty years. The calculator computes a current bond value of $99,495 if interest rates are at 5.01 percent and this is a loss in value of $505 if you sell the twenty-year bond today. Once again the calculator automatically tells you, for comparison, that if yield curve interest rates had moved down 2 full percentage points (200 basis points), you would have gained $29,534 in a sale. If yield curve interest rates had moved up 2 full percentage points, you would have lost $21,943 if you sold the bond. If you retain the twenty-year bond, your portfolio is unaffected except in terms of its **current market value.**

There are several very important lessons to gather from this exercise:

1. The longer the maturity of a bond, the more changes in yield curve interest rates affect its current market value. The value swing of one basis point becomes greater as the time period to maturity and redemption increases.
2. Large moves in interest rates can bring substantial profits (and losses) in bonds sold prior to maturity. So you can have capital gains (and losses) much like stocks with bond investing.
3. With bonds you have income during the time period you are invested, which is generally greater than most dividend-paying or no-dividend stock investments.

Most investors commonly refer to the *value of an "05"* when speaking about bond price fluctuations. What they mean is that this is the preferred unit of measurement of a change in five basis points (.05 percent) of interest rate movement. It is a convenient unit selected because one basis point is a very small number to continually calculate. The current market value of an "05" increases as the maturity of a bond increases because the value swing is larger over the longer number of years until redemption.

UNIQUE BOND-INVESTING METHODS

Here follows some of the methodology of the bond portion of our overall **PLAN**. Some of these pointers are common wisdom, but others do not seem to be referenced in any of the research I have read over the years.

1. Include corporate bonds and taxable bond ETFs, which both have a taxable income stream, inside a tax-sheltered vehicle such as an IRA, Roth IRA, or other qualified tax program, which makes the bond income-tax free until it is withdrawn. This can be a significant advantage due to the miracle of year-after-year compounding, as all of the deferred taxes continue to add to wealth buildup. You can construct a bond ladder if your plan is self-directed and have a municipal bond (think tax-free) ladder in another investment portfolio.

2. Premium bonds, having a coupon yield greater than their yield to maturity, are a problem for some large institutions to buy. Many institutions have no method for accounting for the amortization (disappearance of the amount above $1,000) of the premium paid and tend to buy only bonds that can be acquired at par. This means that the individ-

ual investor can gain a slightly higher yield because there may not be as much competition for the premium bonds. Check with your bond broker.

3. I invested in a combination of premium bonds and zero-coupon bonds, which produced superior cash flow and also kept my principal amount invested intact when the bonds matured. See if you like this concept. It worked for me and I still do it when I can.

If you buy premium bonds and are concerned about their eventual maturity at par, which will be a dollar amount less than you paid for the bond ($1,000 principle plus some amount of premium), there is a way to help correct this problem. Recall that you recouped the premium you paid in the form of increased cash flow over the life of the bond. Still, some investors who have invested X dollars are concerned that in the future they may wish to have X dollars again to invest at the maturity of the bond. You can purchase a zero-coupon bond, which accretes in value to par, at a discount in a matching maturity to the premium bond. At the end of the time period, the accretion on the zero will match fairly closely the amortization of the premium, and you will once again have X dollars to invest.

So let's return to the 5 percent coupon bond that you bought in a 4 percent yield curve market environment. You know that this is a premium bond because it is paying a yearly income of $50 per bond versus the current-market available bonds, which only pay $40 of yearly income. Let's say you paid $1,075 for each bond, which is due in ten years, and bought fifty of them for a total investment of $53,750. That means that in ten years, you will have only $50,000 of principal to reinvest (50 x $1,000 = $50,000) because you got the other $3,750 in cash flow during the life of the bond.

You can also buy fifty zero-coupon bonds, which you know are purchased at a discount, and accrete them to maturity. Let's say you pay $925 for each of your fifty zero-coupon bonds for a total investment of $46,250. All one hundred bonds will mature at par, with the zeros accruing $3,750 over that time, so you will receive back the full $100,000 you invested in both types of bonds in ten years' time and have it available to reinvest.

The reason this works is because zero-coupon bonds pay no yearly income and, in their accretion, the interest on interest is paid at the same rate as when the original bond was purchased. Without the need to reinvest the zero-coupon bond payments, you have no market yield curve risk and know with certainty when the zero-coupon bond matures and is paid off at par.

So you gain a little cash flow from buying a premium bond and lose no principal on the matched investment at maturity. Your overall return is a blend of the yield of the premium bond plus the yield of the zero-coupon bond. A word of reality, however: *you may not always be able to match investment and yield exactly but you can come close most times.* And it may be difficult to locate zero-coupon bonds as they are far rarer than regular bonds. I have found that this strategy works best with municipal bonds, which have a greater supply of both the regular and zero-coupon types.

To do this type of sophisticated investing, you will need a professional bond broker rather than a run-of-the-mill stockbroker who is not likely to be able to locate the bonds you need. It's not hard to make this strategy a common element of your bond portfolio once you have completed the search for an appropriate bond broker. Generally speaking, adopt this strategy once your bond portfolio has grown enough that you can buy in larger lots of fifty to one hundred bonds.

4. Foreign government bonds make a good hedge against declines in value of the dollar. These can readily be purchased in other currencies and then sold at a profit if the other currency gains in strength against the dollar. Some of the richest people in the world made their fortunes doing this kind of investment. It is more speculative than normal municipal and corporate bonds and you should only do it within your risk-tolerance level.

BOND HOLDINGS IN OUR PLAN

Bonds can change in value, sometimes dramatically, but there is always the option of holding to maturity and collecting your par value from a quality bond. Stocks have no guarantee that they will reclaim their value after a precipitous decline.

For my own portfolio, as my family accumulated wealth, we progressively lowered our investment in stocks and relied on bonds as a major investment vehicle. Over a period of approximately twenty years we regularly added pieces to our bond ladder by combining savings from income along with interest earned from other bonds, CDs, stock dividends, and profits from real estate transactions. The more we added in new bonds the larger the income we received, and it began to snowball. By the time I elected to retire at age fifty-four, income from our bond portfolio equaled what my salary used to be as the CEO of a large company. That made the transition out of a work-a-day office to other interests much easier, as it had very little impact on our lifestyle.

That is a crucial part of the philosophy presented in *The Money Plan*. The percentage of bonds versus stocks in our portfolio grew during the first ten years to reflect a decrease in risk tolerance associated with a reduction in my remaining working years. Here are some rough bond ownership guidelines as a percent of overall liquid assets:

OVERALL BOND HOLDINGS AS A PERCENTAGE OF A SAFE AND SECURE PORTFOLIO BY AGE

- Under 35 years old: about 20 percent.
- 35 to 55: about 40 percent of portfolio.
- Over 55 to 65: about 60 percent of portfolio.
- Over 65: about 70 percent of portfolio.

Lest you think these bond percentages are an extreme shift from most investment advisors who have a long-term bias for stocks as the better assets to own, I will refer you to the founder of Pacific Investment Management Company (PIMCO), which has $750 billion under management. Bill Gross, PIMCO's Chief Investment Officer, is one of the legends of investing and is respected worldwide for his conservative asset management ability. He has championed the philosophy that you should hold as little as 30 percent of your portfolio in stocks. I would be content to be at Bill Gross's level of investment savvy anytime. He really is Mr. Bond in word and deed!

3. SUBSECTION: STOCKS

HOW TO MAKE A SMALL FORTUNE IN STOCKS

You know now that I don't really like the notion of picking stocks as the core basis for a wealth-building strategy. Don't misunderstand; I am not saying you should own no stocks. Our *PLAN* just doesn't subscribe to the heavily biased, cultlike use of the stock market espoused by most writers on investments. Stocks, like wine at a meal, are an appropriate part of your portfolio in moderation, although they are much riskier than other asset classes. There is just too much stuff out of your control, and the quirks can blow up your best logic even when you have done your research and should be rewarded. The stocks that have their place in our *PLAN* are in four categories:

1. Large U.S. multinationals of superior quality;
2. Consistent high-dividend-paying companies;
3. New technologies;
4. A few picks with foreign exposure in major companies within other developed economies.

The way many people make a small fortune in the stock market is to start with a large fortune. There are so many irrational variables affecting the price of a company's securities that it is nearly impossible to match cause and effect. It is not uncommon for a company to announce better-than-expected earnings but see analysts trash its public earnings report and recommend selling shares because they feel that the results are too good to continue. Think for a moment. The company succeeds but still its shares may fall in value because an analyst says the happy times can't continue even when the company says they will.

On the other hand, shares of some companies soar because their earnings report states that they *lost less* money than expected, and analysts applaud this development even though the actual performance was awful. They didn't make any profits but shares went up! How can you independently know what to do? You just never know for sure.

At almost any time, general market psychology can overshadow how a company's publicly traded shares would rationally be priced if the stock market were a predictable beast. In other words, *to a great extent the stock market is a crap shoot.* In that sense, it is hard to fit a large exposure to this market into our safe and secure *PLAN*. Most investors in the stock market are born optimists. According to a nationwide survey, the expectation was that U.S. stocks provide a 13.7 percent yearly return. However, the truth according to Ibbotson Associates, a market statistician firm, is that since 1926 U.S. stocks have returned an average of 9.8 percent, or less than 4 percent after adjusting for inflation, taxes, and expenses.

Dozens of ratios are used to describe the relative value of shares in a particular company. The most common is the **Price to Earnings** Ratio (P/E), which is a measure of the price paid for a share of stock as compared to the annual net income (or profit) earned per share. The higher the P/E, the more investors pay for a unit of a company's earnings. Each industry has its own P/E average. For example, high-tech companies have a much higher P/E in general than basic steel companies. This is because investors expect their technology sales and earnings to increase rapidly, whereas the basic steel company is likely to plod along with fairly constant sales and earnings. While that's the theory, it's often not always the actuality.

MORE ON CHARTISTS

FOR STOCKS AND their markets there are numerous technical analysts who spend their days in search of price and volume patterns they can deduce from specific market data. These *chartists* believe they can draw insights into either the direction of a particular stock or the overall movement likely in the near future of financial markets. A chartist often relates indicators to each other that he believes work in tandem or opposition in a *chart*. Most are done with *moving averages,* meaning that they plot the average price over a specified period of time (usually twenty, thirty, fifty, one hundred, and two hundred days). In general, the shorter the time period selected, the more volatile the moving average indicator as longer periods tend to smooth out smaller, rapid fluctuations. The conclusion derived from the trend is then used as a basis for buying or selling investments. For example, Dow Theory tracks the relationship between the Dow Industrials and Dow Transport moving averages, believing that this interaction predicts overall Dow Jones Industrial Average movement. Other chartists/analysts track things like the ten-year Japanese government bond yields to the Dow Jones transportation average. Some chartists only follow a single variable such as the movement of consumer prices.

A chart of a stock often has a ***resistance level*** where the rising price tends to slow down, stop, or bounce off of an upper limit. However, once it is broken through (meaning investors will pay more than the resistance price), there is usually significant upward movement until a new resistance level is established. A ***support level*** is the opposite of a resistance level and may indicate where new buyers will enter the market to establish a new position in a security or other holders may add more, cheaper shares to an older position. However, once a stock price has broken through a support level (meaning fallen below it), the price tends to continue to trend lower until at some point additional buyers are willing to acquire cheaper shares at the lower level.

Charts are useful tools but not wholly reliable. The reason is simple: past behavior is not an entirely accurate predictor of future behavior. If you want to learn more about charting, www.stockcharts.com has multiple blogs with charting information and even has a chart school. s always, www.wikipedia.com is useful for definitions and more general reference.

Here is a funny part of the stock market. Sometimes things work as they rationally should: shareholders are rewarded with steady increases in market capitalization with a higher stock price or expanded P/E that reflects improving results. That is the textbook case of how it should be. But in general, it's very similar to golf, where you shoot seventeen horrible holes and swear you are giving up the game. Then you hit off the tee on the eighteenth hole to within six inches of the pin, and that one shot makes you feel like you finally understand how to play. Stock pickers and golfers keep coming back because of that once-in-a-while winning moment.

MARGIN CREDIT

IN OUR SAFE and secure posture, we never use *margin credit* to buy investments. Margin credit means you use borrowed money, usually from your broker, to pay for part of the stock purchase. As with any loan, the magnified effect of margin losses in a downturn can sink the whole program—and then some. If you buy a $30 stock and borrow $20 of each share purchased, should a downturn occur and the stock price decline to $20, your equity is wiped out. And you will pay interest on the borrowed $20 as long as the loan is outstanding.

At no point in my financial life was more than 40 percent of my net worth tied to the stock market, and the more wealth my family accumulated the lower the overall percentage became. The percentage of stock exposure also reduced with age to reflect a decrease in risk profile associated with a reduction in the working years left to recoup a loss. Some industry analysts suggest that the percentage of stocks in your overall financial portfolio should equal 110 (or some advisors pick 100) minus your age. My percentage number is considerably lower. Here are my rough percentage stock-exposure guidelines including domestic and foreign securities as a percent of your total assets:

OVERALL STOCK HOLDINGS AS A PERCENTAGE OF A SAFE AND SECURE PORTFOLIO BY AGE

- Under 35 years old: up to 50 percent
- 35 to 55 years old: up to 25 percent
- 55 to 70 years old: up to 15 percent
- Over 70 years old: less than 10 percent

The best kind of decisions to make in the stock market are of lower-tier risk. Recall the words of Charles Schwab on his poor experience with hot tips. A more valid approach is to ride an informed belief in the direction of a trend, such as interest rates rising or falling; understand that war demands force government spending in a certain industry; believing in a young industry that is about to mature (flat-screen TVs, computers, chips, Internet, medical breakthroughs); standing apart without irrational fear that others possess and is likely to fade away (wording awkward here) (after Black Monday or 9/11); or believing an economy is recovering nicely from a recession. Another approach is to select a company with a compelling product that is not yet widely appreciated but that you have used and feel it is likely to succeed. (One of the most successful portfolio managers at Fidelity used this technique.) But for our *PLAN* and your portfolio, invest on the long side, meaning that you own the shares of a company or the trend itself in some form such as a stock, mutual fund, ETF, or SPDR.

The idea of *short selling* a company's stock, or selling shares you do not own in hopes of the price falling and buying it more cheaply, never appealed to *safe and secure* as the exposure is unlimited if the price keeps going up. That kind of gamble is for stock professionals.

SHORT PROFITS ARE A TALL ORDER

IN MOST CASES investors direct their energies into finding companies whose prospects will improve. That change will be reflected in a rising share value and create investor profit as the worth of the enterprise grows. More and higher quality earnings translate into an expanding price-to-earnings ratio. An arithmetic jump also occurs from the multiplication of a larger earnings-per-share dollar amount times the company's price-to-earnings ratio.

For example, if a company is earning $1.50 per share of stock outstanding and has a P/E ratio of 15 times forward earnings, its stock may trade at around $22.50 per share ($1.5 x 15 = $22.50). However, if the company has grown significantly, two things may happen. First, more investors may want to own shares and the increased demand might move the P/E ratio from 15 to perhaps 20 times forward earning. Second, the company may actually earn more income, translating, for our example, to $2.25 per share outstanding. Calculating with these new values gives us a share price of $45.00 ($2.25 x 20 = $45.00). That is called *being long a stock* and is how most investors buy shares. Note that all that is at risk are the funds that have been paid for the shares.

Some investors seek out companies whose business will weaken and earn less income per share. Short sellers bet on this happening; this is called *shorting a stock*. This type of transaction does not fit into our safe and secure PLAN. In order to short a stock, you must sell shares you do not own, after borrowing them from someone who lends them for a fee. You sell these borrowed shares at what you believe is a high price in the hope of buying them back in the market at a lower price and returning the borrowed shares to the original owner. If you are wrong and the price of the shares continues to climb, there is no limit on your potential loss as there is no ceiling on how high the price can rise.

Short selling must always be done in a margin account where the short seller posts a percentage of the price (currently 50 percent) of the value of the borrowed shares. The brokerage firm then lends the difference to create leverage (and we have discussed several times how borrowed money can magnify a gain or a loss). The short seller is now paying a fee to the original owner of the shares plus a fee to the broker.

For example, if one thousand shares of a stock are shorted at $40 per share, the short seller would need to have $20,000 in the margin account. Those thousand shares would have to be sold for $40,000 to have proceeds of $60,000 in the margin account as collateral for the short sale. Each night when the market closes, the margin account must have 50 percent of the value of the shares. This is called *marking to market* the short trade. If the stock should double in price to $80 per share instead of fall, the short seller would have to post more money in the margin account or have the brokerage firm buy the $80 shares in the market and return them to the share lender. The loss in that case would be all of the original $20,000 plus another $20,000 for the difference between the $60,000 in the margin account and the $80,000 it cost to buy back the thousand shares (1,000 x $80 = $80,000). The loss would be a total of $40,000 plus fees and interest.

There have been many situations in which short sellers have tried to hold on to a short position by continuing to post more and more money in hopes that a particular stock price would eventually decline. I can think of a recent case where a $45 stock kept rising until it got into the $300-per-share range (including subsequent stock splits). Those short sellers at the $45 level had an almost limitless loss. Shorting is a danger zone where a stock can unexpectedly skyrocket and do great financial harm. That is why, for the portion of your portfolio exposed to the stock market, being long a stock (in other words, owning shares and being bullish on the company) is the most appropriate and prudent course of investment for our PLAN.

Some financial experts will take issue with my long side attitude and conservative weighting of stocks. Many of them recommend that younger investors have 60–80 percent or more of investable funds in the stock market and specify it be invested in growth areas. Perhaps they see something that I have missed over the years. However, as the *PLAN*'s success in investing in good and bad markets proves, not too many opportunities have passed me by. Our safe and secure posture eschews such large stock exposure as too much speculation.

There are a few techniques to mitigate some portion of the gamble associated with stocks. We have already discussed *diversification*. Other methods include special ETFs, SPYDRs, puts and calls, futures, mutual funds, stop orders, charting, contrarian stock picking, and a longer list of esoteric instruments we can ignore. We will touch upon some of these strategies as we concentrate on lower-risk profiles and building free cash flow. Each one requires a good deal of study and attention for its mitigation of equity risk to have any real effect. No single one is the magic bullet.

The five most dangerous words in investing are,
"This stock technique always works."

STOCK MESSAGE BOARDS

MANY PUBLICLY TRADED companies have Internet sites where normal shareholders can post comments about events that might affect stock price. Find out where by going to www.Yahoo.com or www.google.com and entering the symbol of a company to get to their home page. Then access their company message board for your personal entertainment and often a really unbelievable read. In my experience there are four kinds of shareholder message board contributors:

1. Those who know very little.
2. Those who don't know much but are somewhat aware of their limitations.
3. Those who have no clue that they don't know or understand anything.
4. Those who try to manipulate the stock.

Shareholder message boards are not a source of reliable investment information. Don't use them as a basis for any of your investment decisions. Some professional shorts (bear investors who only bet on stock declines) try to make money by crashing the price of a stock they have shorted and borrowed in the hope of buying it more cheaply to return to the lender. It is not uncommon for bears to pay others to constantly post negative comments about a company they have shorted—and even to make up and spread malicious rumors. Here's an investment message: stay away from advice on message boards! This part of the market is a rigged game and message boards are part of it.

4. MUTUAL FUNDS

A **mutual fund** is an investment vehicle that sells shares to the public and then invests the proceeds in a diversified portfolio of stocks, bonds, or other financial instruments. There are several benefits to a mutual fund: it is relatively liquid since the shares can readily be bought and sold; a "professional" manager is supposed to be working full-time on the portfolio; a mutual fund is convenient; and in many cases it allows for automatic reinvestment of dividends so the miracle of compounding can do its work. The disadvantage is that all of these benefits come with fees. There are often upfront fees, or **loads** (1–4 percent plus), management fees (0.25–3 percent each year), and redemption or **back-end fees** (0.25–1 percent). They all eat into your investment returns. In addition, the larger funds are not very nimble, since they have a lot of money and no single investment success will have a dramatic effect on performance. As a method to achieve diversity without the effort of making individual asset picks, a mutual fund comes at a price. But it may serve as a good vehicle for investors who do not have enough capital to achieve their own diverse portfolio or for those who are just starting to build a financial plan.

If you are going to include a mutual fund portion in your universal financial portfolio, I advise you to stick with **no-load** and

low-load funds. These funds do not charge a fee, or only charge a small one, when you buy or sell shares. More money put to work earlier in your investment cycle can make a huge difference in your net return over time. If you pay a fee of 2–4 percent just to buy a fund, that puts only 96–98 percent of your investable funds to work. Those fees will significantly diminish your compounded returns over a long period of time. Ignore a broker who gets a good portion of the fee and wants to steer you into his "favorite" high-performing load fund. There are many excellent no-load funds from which to choose.

There are two broad categories of mutual funds: **closed-end** and **open-end**.

Closed-end funds make a single sale to the public to raise capital, after which the fund itself will not sell or redeem shares. After the initial offering, closed-end investors create the **secondary market** value of a share by bidding for or selling their shares. That means subsequent sales can be above, or in many cases well below, the underlying net asset value of a closed-end mutual fund. Obviously when the price is well below, you are not receiving the real value for your investment as if it were priced at the true net asset value. That added exposure is not very attractive for the average investor who purchases at the offering. However, it can be an attractive opportunity to a subsequent purchaser who buys in at the discounted price after the offering. With closed-end funds you have the underlying risk of the assets themselves, with the added risk of demand or lack thereof for buying and selling shares if you wish to purchase more or redeem. However, closed-end funds may be traded throughout the day at certain prices in a secondary market (a market in which an investor purchases a security from another investor rather than the issuer—if there are investors willing to buy them. There are two free Web sites to learn more about closed-end funds: www.closed-endfunds. com, maintained by the Closed-End Fund Association, and www.

cefconnect.com sponsored by the Nuveen Investment fund manager. Nuveen also has a free kit with more information.

Open-ended funds are constantly accessible to sell shares to new or previous investors at the closing price of the net asset value on any given day. The open-ended fund itself is available to redeem shares if you wish to sell, so it more closely mirrors its true value. You may accomplish dollar-cost averaging relatively easily and efficiently since adding to your position is as simple as calling the fund or going online.

Mutual funds come in so many varieties that people use the concept for just about every purpose. Here follows a partial list:

- Municipal bond funds:
  - Long, medium, or short maturities
  - Tax free
  - State specific
- Corporate bond funds
- Government bond funds
- Index funds
- Life-cycle funds (all your assets are allocated with a target maturity at retirement)
- Balanced funds (some income and moderate appreciation)
- Sector funds (one industry segment)
- Growth funds (aggressive capital appreciation)
- Money market funds
- Commodity funds
- Income funds
- Emerging market funds
- Fund of funds
- Green earth funds
- Religious-based investments

There are about eight thousand U.S.-based mutual funds. Before you buy any fund it is important to read the prospectus and get a feel for how the fund operates. Just about anything you need to know is in the prospectus. I don't read every word but rather concentrate on the defined goals of the mutual fund: fees, a glance at the portfolio, historic returns, and the track record of the manager. Then I look at financial publications such as *Forbes*, *Bloomberg Business Week*, and *Kiplinger's Personal Finance*, each of which have ratings systems to evaluate individual fund performance.

The Internet has a wealth of information on mutual funds. You can find rankings of performance, analyst reviews, and graphs of virtually any mutual fund and its returns over time. Go to www. Yahoo.com/finance and set up a personal portfolio using the symbols for each of your mutual funds (you can also add any stocks you own). I also add a second portfolio of funds or stocks I am thinking about buying or selling so that I can follow their price movement over time. Yahoo lets you create as many personal portfolios as you want. Bookmark these pages in "favorites" on your computer and check them often to see how your choices are progressing. This simple action will keep you in touch with the market and your money.

In addition, a great, highly credible source of information on mutual funds is www.Morningstar.com, where you can find out about the largest funds, the top no-load funds, five-star-rated funds, and funds with the best year-to-date performance. Morningstar also has a research subscription service. Your broker may be able to furnish some of this information at no cost to you.

I also like to look at the trend on a fifty-two-week moving average on funds for its long-range perspective. Visit www.contrarianprofits.com for a short article on how moving averages can help you do better investing. All moving averages smooth out the bumps that occur in financial markets to give you the bigger picture. A fifty-two-week chart is always updated with the latest performance information to keep you current.

My favorite fund families are **Fidelity** (www.FidelityInvestments. com), **Legg Mason** (www.leggmason.com), and **Vanguard** (www. Vanguard.com), although there are many other fine families of funds. Both Fidelity and Vanguard have great telephone service, easy-to-follow statements, and their size and stability assure your assets to be *safe and secure* as called for in the first leg of our financial stool. They also provide a large selection of mutual fund offerings and make it easy to switch within their internal funds. Fidelity publishes a newsletter that is helpful, but still somewhat slanted toward its own funds. In recent years Fidelity has made most of its fee structure competitive.

Vanguard is the king of no-load investing, with very low yearly management fees and excellent "buy-the-market" funds. When we discussed stocks, I said that most of my stock investing was along the lines of buying my hunches on a broad economic trend. Examples of this are the expectation of returning inflation from government overspending leading to higher interest rates, or a new administration that is business and Wall Street friendly, which often means rising stock markets. Buying an index fund of any type is one method of riding a trend with limited capital and exposure.

Vanguard has a Total Stock Market Index, Small Cap Value Index, European Stock Index, All World Ex-US Stock Index, High Dividend Yield Index, and 500 Index among many other offerings. These funds are passively managed, meaning they don't require research because they include a specific group of securities and infrequently trade individual positions. They buy set investment offerings and hold them. The investor is in effect buying the diversified basket of the contents without having to go out and buy each issue individually. Because they don't require an expensive manager and staff, their very low expenses mean very low fees. Fidelity has some of the same sort of mutual funds and is lowering its fees to compete better on index funds, but mostly has actively managed offerings with higher expenses and fees.

You need not limit yourself to the Fidelity and Vanguard families but should have a pretty compelling reason to buy elsewhere—and the fact that a fund had turbo-charged performance last year is not a compelling reason. Buying into one of those past year champions is almost always a loser's game. When they say past performance is no guarantee of future performance, they mean it. Study what has happened over five, ten, and fifteen years in a mutual fund and then decide if you need to own it.

MUTUAL FUND RESEARCH

FORBES PUBLISHES THE kind of research that you cannot do yourself, because of time and information-access constraints, at www.forbes.com. Before buying a mutual fund, read a Forbes special issue on Honor Roll Winners, identifying funds and fund managers "that not only make assets grow in good times but also protect them in bad ones." I save that issue each year and refer to it. A word of caution though: it is unwise to simply buy the Forbes yearly Honor Roll list blindly. Some funds do drop off the list and others are simply not suited to your universal portfolio or risk-tolerance level. *Business Week* also has several quality issues that rank mutual funds and their investment potential (www.businessweek.com). Comparing the two publications may provide some additional insight.

If you determine that mutual funds are in your financial future, they should make up no more than half of the stock percentage guidelines we covered in the last chapter. And avoid bond mutual funds in favor of owning the individual bonds. Such bond funds are usually a bad bet compared to your own well-thought-out bond portfolio.

So here is how the rubber meets the road with respect to mutual fund investing. In our *PLAN* it is not necessary to avoid mutual funds, but I am not a great fan of overusing them. Here are the top ten reasons to be cautious:

1. *Funds that charge a fee.* You're working hard and you're frugal, so you'll have a comfortable $1million-plus nest egg when you retire. Your thought is to take out $40,000 per year from that nest egg and supplement it with income from Social Security for, say, another $14,000 per year. You are investing in mutual funds, which have an industry average annual fee of 1.6 percent. When you retire, the government will take approximately $3,365 in federal taxes (state and local taxes are additional) for ordinary income tax and slightly less if part of your income is capital gains.

   You complain to all your friends about the greedy government. Meanwhile, if your mutual fund fees on the $1 million nest egg are 1.6 percent, you will pay the fund manager $16,000 per year, or four times what you pay to Uncle Sam! That is why a prudent investor buys only no-load and low-annual-fee mutual funds. Plus, as we have already discussed, lower fees leave more money in your account to continue the miracle of compounding for a very tidy profit.

   When it comes to enriching itself at the expense of its investors, the mutual fund industry has few equals. The average expense ratio is 0.81 percent and produces some $89 billion in income for the $11 trillion mutual fund industry.

2. *Fund managers.* Fund managers are normally paid by how well the mutual fund performs in any given year. They are human, just like you. If there is a big downturn in the market and a lot of gloomy reactionaries choose to get out near the bottom, the fund manager must sell securities to meet the redemption notices. The manager is likely to sell the winners in the fund prematurely and thereby preserve her bonus. The flip side is that she may hang on to clunker investments longer because they will not raise as much cash to pay for redemptions.

3. *Mutual fund share classes.* Mutual funds may offer more than one class of their shares to investors. Many have A, B, and C classes, with the principal difference being the fees and expenses associated with the class. If you haven't read the fine print in the prospectus, which is often more complex than Relativity Theory, you might end up with less than you bargained for. You can do a quick check on fees through Morningstar, Google, or the Security and Exchange Commission's Web site. Go to the Investor Information section of www.sec.gov/investor/ to review the SEC's Mutual Funds Costs.

4. *Overinvested mutual funds.* A mutual fund may be bound not to have more than 5–10 percent of its assets in cash (some are required to be "fully invested") even when it is not wise to own securities due to market conditions. Shareholders may not be protected and suffer extra and unnecessary harm.

5. *Poor short-term performance.* Half of the mutual funds perform in the lower half of their peer group. You don't want the cardiac surgeon who graduated in the lower half of his class operating on your heart. You also don't want the lower half of performing mutual funds managing your money.

6. *Poor long-term performance.* Only 10 percent of the funds handily top the passive S&P500 Index over long periods of time. Meaning, if the overall market rose 7 percent, then 90 percent of all mutual funds did the same 7 percent gain, or worse, and you would have been better off with a vanilla Index Fund that just tracked the market because of its much lower fee structure.

7. *Uncontrolled growth.* Successful mutual funds attract too much cash and grow large very quickly. This drags on performance because the manager may not be able to locate acceptable investments to sustain the previous level of returns. You may be forced to sell, pay taxes, and move on.

8. *Sales go through at end of day only.* In a major market crash, if you decide to sell, your mutual fund trade is not put through until the 4:00 PM closing bell of the market. And that is a "ding dong, the witch is dead" moment. Only you are the witch. Mutual funds do not, as a general rule, trade intraday, so you watch as the value declines with no other option. The reverse scenario is equally true: you may miss out on a major market upswing.

9. *Fund merging.* Many poorly performing funds are merged into better-performing ones to make the overall family of funds appear to perform better than it actually does.

10. *Fund overlap.* Many mutual fund portfolios overlap, so you may believe you are getting diversity but in fact are not. www.Morningstar.com has an Instant X-Ray tool where you can enter symbols and see how your investments are distributed for diversification safety.

When some people get older they no longer want to, or are able to, do the work necessary to manage their money. For funds that are committed at the money manager's discretion (called a **discretionary account**), employ an individual who has worked a long while with the family. He or she is likely to select mutual funds or stocks with your tolerance for risk in mind. I also favor older advisors who will tend to listen to their own ideas and perhaps incorporate them into the portfolio. Their fees are comparable to those of mutual fund managers (1–1.5 percent per year) and, in some cases, lower. Money managers also negotiate to lower fees for larger investors. In effect, they create a custom mutual fund probably closely aligned to a family's needs. Such a custom portfolio should be able to convert to a very high cash position at any point to pay estate taxes, meet medical expenses, or otherwise to protect assets

5. ETFs, SPDRs, etc.

ETFS, SPDRS, AND MLPS

I generally do not subscribe to the latest and greatest fad in investing and that has steered me away from things like derivatives, which devastated the worldwide financial markets in 2008–2009. However, during the last two decades one advance that is worth some study as part of your diversification of investments is the **exchange-traded fund (ETF).** ETFs are perhaps the most useful financial product to be recently developed in the marketplace in many years because of their versatility and ability to customize specific investing objectives. At the present moment there is more than $1 trillion held in ETFs, and the amount is rising daily.

Standard & Poor's Depositary Receipts (*SPDRs*), called "Spyders"in the financial press, are not arachnids in spite of their funny name. They are shares of a brand of ETFs managed by State Street Global Advisors (and a few other firms) and are designed to track various indexes. SPDRs trade on the stock exchange under the symbol "SPY." In this section we will go into some detail on specific uses for ETFs that make sense for a conservative investor.

ETFs are kissing cousins of mutual funds except that they trade on stock exchanges in the same manner as regular stocks. They are a blend between a stock and a mutual fund; they provide a healthy measure of the diversification that the safe and secure philosophy of our PLAN demands; they can be bought and sold all day long; and if you choose to own stocks they can make up the core of your holdings. ETFs hold assets such as public stocks, commodities, global market indexes, portions of stock indexes, esoteric instruments, industry sectors, precious metals, direct investment in specific countries, bonds, and much more in similar fashion to a mutual fund. But ETFs adjust their net asset value intraday to allow for buying and selling during the normal course of market trading hours. They possess continuous liquidity. And we understand the importance of liquidity to a healthy financial strategy. When markets are changing rapidly, tradability is a very valuable feature.

That continuous intraday trading gives them a major stocklike benefit as opposed to the pricing policy of most open-end mutual funds that calculate net asset value only at the closing bell. That's too late to react to good or bad news and you must wait for the opening bell to take action. Here are some methodologies and reasons to consider ETFs:

1. COMMISSIONS AND ETF EXPENSES

In general the commissions for buying and selling ETFs have been about the same as stocks, but that is rapidly changing. At the time of writing this book, Charles Schwab, Fidelity, and Vanguard allow the trading of many exchange-traded funds without commissions. This makes it economic to do dollar-cost averaging and make additions and deletions to your portfolio without fees reducing the amount you have invested. It is quite likely this trend will continue. An additional benefit is the costs associated with owning ETFs are dramatically lower than in most mutual funds. An actively traded mutual fund, on average, has an annual expense of about 1.42 percent whereas ETFs that are very similar may cost around 0.48 percent a year. Think about how positive that additional savings is for the miracle of compounding.

2. TAX CONTROL

The tax efficiency of ETFs derives from the fact that they are constructed to tightly track an index and thus have very low investment turnover. If an investor wants out of an ETF, he simply sells the shares into the market to another investor with no effect on the basic portfolio of the ETF. That means the ETF will rarely experience capital gains from a change of assets like an actively traded mutual fund that buys and sells many times to accommodate redemptions and purchases. Since mutual funds do not pay taxes themselves, they are obligated to distribute capital gains to all shareholders who then have to pay the taxes individually. ETFs act more like a regular stock, so they generate less unwanted capital gains to pass on to shareholders. However, an ETF does reflect the securities it owns, so dividend distributions from underlying stock and interest on bonds will still be passed on to your tax return. Also, ETFs that hold gold or other precious metals, such as the very popular **SPDR GOLD SHARES (GLD),** are taxed like collectibles on their gains (currently 28 percent) versus normal capital gains tax (currently 15 percent).

Ordinarily, if you wish for tax purposes to take advantage of a stock loss you have to sell it and may not repurchase it for thirty-one days. But ETFs offer a way of accomplishing this without the problem of discontinuity. Let's say you purchased the shares of XYZ Company the day before it had a major problem that caused the price to fall significantly. You are convinced the situation will be solved and the company shares will rebound and increase in value. You might sell the XYZ Company shares, capture the loss for tax purposes, and buy an ETF that has the XYZ Company as a major holding. You would still participate for those thirty-one days in owning the XYZ Company. At the end of thirty-one days, the ETF could be sold and you may repurchase the XYZ Company shares with no disruption in the asset allocation you had planned. In addition, the loss for tax purposes may be used to offset other gains … and that is real profit left in your pocket!

3. SIMPLE ETF INVESTING

We have already mentioned mutual funds that enable you to buy a sector, the whole, or a major segment, of the market. ETFs can do the same thing and they provide additional benefits. The most commonly purchased ETFs are designed to track certain benchmark indexes such as:

Dow Jones Industrial Average
Dow Jones Commodity Index
Emerging Market Index
Russell 2000 Index
Standard & Poor's 500 Stock Index
MSCI World
Standard & Poor's Global 100
Wilshire 5000
Nikkei 250 (Tokyo Stock Exchange)
FTSI 100 (UK Companies)

There are several different firms that offer their own version of an ETF for each of the above benchmarks, and new ones are appearing all the time.

You can buy an ETF in order to invest your funds so that they earn a profit as a benchmark average moves up in value. There are other ETFs that are constructed to profit from the opposite decline of a benchmark index. There are even ETFs that are trying to perform better than a traditional benchmark using leverage, but our safe and secure strategy does not recommend this kind of choice.

4. TACTICAL ETF INVESTING

Unlike individual stocks, ETFs can be used to bet on a market sector without the need for you to be correct about the prospects of a particular company. It is very difficult to pinpoint the winner out of a group of companies. Let's say you are certain that the health-care sector will do well in the coming years but are unsure as to which company will prosper most. It is easy to find an ETF that has the health-care sector as its focus and invest in a fashion similar to a sector mutual fund. The difference is that you will avoid the common load charges, high yearly management fees, and may even be able to buy the ETF with no commission. This will not relieve you of the same sort of research suggested about a mutual fund investigation; pay attention to the company composition, choose a reputable ETF firm, and periodically review your ETF's progress.

Some ETF experts advocate an equal sector investment strategy for ETF investment. In this method your portfolio is divided into five—nine sector ETFs with an equal proportion of investable funds placed in each one.

Doing this gives meaningful exposure to a wide part of the market so that you can participate in whatever industry rallies occur because of this diversification. Keep in mind this tactic is a substitute for the stock market portion of your portfolio and is not the major focus of safe and secure. Mr. Bonds is still the overall winner in our lifetime **PLAN** to get rich slowly.

5. BOND ETF INVESTING

ETFs can be used to build a custom bond portfolio since there are funds that invest in taxable municipal bonds, corporate bonds, various government bonds, overseas bonds, sovereign debt, and mortgages. A diversified portfolio of these assets can be a part of your overall strategy along with your bond ladder. It is even possible to hedge your bets against interest rate rises by adding an inverse ETF bond fund that is designed to rise as the price of treasury securities falls. Another way to fight rising interest rates as well as inflation is to buy an ETF that invests in **treasury inflation-protected securities (TIPS)**. This very specialized ETF is likely to hold its value better than owning standard treasury Bonds outright, but you will sacrifice some cash flow for the protection.

6. MASTER LIMITED PARTNERSHIPS

Another useful diversification for your portfolio is Master Limited Partnerships (*MLPs*), which often offer high dividends and also trade like stocks. They combine the tax benefits of a limited partnership with the liquidity of a publicly traded security. MLPs are generally in the natural-resource business and pay a required (by regulation) quarterly dividend that is a set amount. The vast majority are in the pipeline business, which tends to have stable income from the transport of gas or oil. They avoid corporate tax because they are a partnership and also allow investors to share in depreciation (which reduces your tax liability from other investments). There is an excellent primer for MLPs at http://www.alerian. com/MLPprimer.pdf (dead link--would not open). Some examples of MLPs are Kinder Morgan Energy Partners (symbol: KMP) and Plains All American Pipeline LP (symbol: PAA).

There is a wealth of information on the Internet at www.google.com or www.bing.com about ETFs, SPDRs, and MLPs. It is easy to access and clearly presented, as these diversification tools are widely used. Most brokerage firms like Fidelity Investments, Charles Schwab, UBS, and others also have printed material on this subject. As always, do your homework to become informed before committing hard-earned money to your selected strategy. Let's now consider three portfolios that could make use of them.

THE THREE BEARS' MUTUAL FUND/ETF PORTFOLIOS

Goldilocks is an investment advisor who loves our safe and secure **PLAN**. As a general rule, Goldilocks will not feed the portfolios of the three bears with the latest meal that Wall Street has cooked up. And she knows some bears like it dished out with moderate risk, other bears like it with less risk, and some bears like mostly income so they can go out to eat without an upset stomach.

Almost everyone with assets has a list of different smaller portfolios in their overall financial **PLAN**. You and your spouse may have a traditional IRA, a Roth IRA, and a 401(k), so right there you have six accounts. Then there will be college funds for children, funds for a specific major future purchase (vacation home, trip, etc.), and a host of possible trust and charitable portfolios. In some of these cases, mutual funds are an acceptable way to go. If your 401(k) is with an employer, the choices are all likely to be mutual funds so there is no way out of selecting investments from the approved list. Only the percentage allocation among types is in your control.

So let's see how the three bears allocated their stock market money in our **PLAN** when Goldilocks came by to help them with their individual universal portfolios. Papa Bear wanted something designed for his more aggressive growth objectives. Mama Bear was more modest, wanting a balanced design stressing capital preservation and current income with modest growth. Baby Bear wanted a portfolio designed for long-term growth that increased value over time with a lot of diversification within funds. Here is how Goldilocks constructed a portfolio of mutual funds and/or Exchange Traded Funds (ETF) that can be used with or in place of mutual funds to meet each bear's needs.

– CHART 7.4 –
PAPA BEAR: MORE AGGRESSIVE GROWTH

TYPE OF MUTUAL FUND/ETF	PERCENTAGE ALLOCATION
Value fund (1) or ETF	10
Emerging markets fund or ETF	5
International index fund or ETF	5
Financial sector fund or ETF	10
Mid-cap growth fund or ETF	10
Total stock market index fund or ETF	40
NASDAQ 100 fund or ETF	20

(1) Value Mutual Funds tend to focus on safety rather than growth and often choose investments providing excellent dividends as well as some capital appreciation.

The defining characteristics of Papa Bear's aggressive growth objective are a larger exposure to the domestic and international stock markets and no attempt to produce income from his portfolio. He has also slanted his stocks toward the smaller NASDAQ companies rather than the larger and more established household names that often comprise a large-cap fund. Papa Bear is counting on rapid smaller company growth to aid him in capital appreciation and has a concentration in the financial sector that can have very large moves up . . .and down.

– CHART 7.5 –
MAMA BEAR: BALANCED GROWTH

TYPE OF MUTUAL FUND/ETF	PERCENTAGE ALLOCATION
International stock fund or ETF	5.0
NASDAQ 100 fund or ETF	15.0
Total stock market index fund or ETF	32.5
Large-cap growth fund or ETF	7.5
Treasury bond fund or ETF	15.0
Short-term corporate bond fund or ETF	10.0
Value fund or ETF	12.5
Energy index sector fund or ETF	2.5

Mama Bear has balanced her portfolio between her exposure to stocks and a desire to produce current income from bond funds. Also, her large-cap stocks are likely to provide an additional source of dividend income along with modest growth.

– CHART 7.6 –
BABY BEAR: LONG-TERM GROWTH

TYPE OF MUTUAL FUND/ETF	PERCENTAGE ALLOCATION
International growth fund or ETF	10
Various sector fund choices or ETFs	20
NASDAQ fund or ETF	15
Total stock market index fund or ETF	30
Emerging market fund or ETF	5
Corporate bond fund or ETF	5
Commodities fund or ETF	5
Value fund or ETF	10

Baby Bear's long-term growth objective also exposes her to stock market fluctuations and has a minor income component. Although emerging markets have great potential, they are not as developed as the U.S. markets. But Baby Bear has the time to wait for them to grow and solidify.

All three bears have diversified themselves so as to have international as well as domestic stock market exposure, large cap and smaller cap positions, and some index exposure.

None of these mutual fund portfolios is gospel. Depending on the risk and diversity of other assets in your total portfolio, you can play with the percentages allocated to each type of investment objective. As master of your own ship, you must review and rate all your picks at least twice each year. The guidelines above are suggested diversifications for keeping as safe and secure as possible within the most applicable investment objective that fits into your risk-tolerance level. Goldilocks can't do it all for you.

6. REAL ESTATE

HOME SWEET HOME

For most people the cornerstone of their investment portfolio is their home—a house, condominium, town house, cooperative, or other residential unit. Some of the "experts" on capital formation will say that a family should not consider their home as an investment. For my money, this view is rather shortsighted and pretty far from the reality of wealth creation. You may consider a home (or several homes) the foundation of a family fortune as long as you plan for it, do not overreach in what you purchase, are relatively correct in its value in relation to the market, and choose a location that is both convenient and somewhat stable in value. Sure, it is an illiquid investment, but that does not mean it has no place in your portfolio. Houses are a store of wealth and a quality-of-life addition.

At the present time some 70 percent of Americans own a home, and most went through a long exercise of financial planning in its acquisition. Before you go out looking or hire a broker, determine what you can afford to pay based on your income as well as the assets you have already accumulated as a down payment. If you are following our **PLAN**, you should have been saving 20–50 percent of your income and reinvesting the earnings on it. With the miracle of compound investing you should have a substantial, and growing, nest egg at your disposal.

Most people need a mortgage loan to purchase their first home and we have already discussed guidelines for that transaction. There are dozens of different kinds of mortgages (fixed rate, five- or ten-year adjustable rate, etc.), which we won't discuss here because the products offered by lenders are constantly changing.

You can easily do the research about mortgages online at sites like www.QuickenLoan.com or www.mortgage101.com.

In terms of monthly mortgage payments, most lenders have a test that requires the monthly bill sent to the borrower to be no more than 28 to 40 percent of *gross income*. Gross income is what you make before taxes and other deductions are taken out. Lenders also consider your total housing costs that may include such items as property insurance, heat, real estate taxes, along with other outstanding monthly debt payments.

▶ HOW MUCH DOWN PAYMENT DO I NEED?

The ideal amount to put down on a home is 25 percent, but this depends on the market in which you are purchasing. In certain areas of California, a minimal home will cost in the area of $600,000 with $150,000 as a down payment. Let's return to the concept of *future value* and assume that your combined family income, with two working spouses, is $100,000 per year and you are saving approximately $20,000 to $30,000 per year after taxes in an investment portfolio returning 7 percent on average. Let's also assume that you have a rainy-day fund separate from your investment portfolio. Starting from scratch you can compute the years needed for a future value of $150,000 using one of Google's online calculators. Plug in the numbers and compute that it will take approximately four-and-a-half to five years to save up for the $150,000 down payment at $20,000 to $30,000 a year. Of course your income is likely to rise during that time period, and if you save the increased income it will accelerate the accumulation of the down payment. You will forego the benefit of the extra spendable income for a larger goal of home ownership.

You may decide that a less expensive area, where homes are selling for a more reasonable price, is a better bet for a first-home purchase. In many locations a very nice starter home will cost in the range of $250,000 with a down payment of $62,500. You could handle that amount in under three years assuming the same 7 percent return. Perhaps such locations are the better choice for beginning the real-estate portion of your wealth-building program, assuming you can find similar employment there.

▶ SHOULD I BUY A HANDYMAN'S SPECIAL?

One way to stretch your dollars further is to buy a *handyman's special*: a home that needs some work and updating. A large portion of this labor can be your own sweat equity, so you may get a larger house that you fix up over time. As a method of wealth accumulation, my family bought, fixed up, and resold five homes. We spent about two years in each home and worked on them evenings and weekends. Our children helped out, learning repair skills and the value of hard work as our family net worth rapidly increased. We never used the profits for other purposes besides home investment, making a larger down payment for each successive home. Although we kept buying more expensive homes in better neighborhoods, our mortgage amount remained relatively constant because of the expanding equity. This strategy only works if you do not form an emotional attachment to these homes but rather view them as investments.

By the time we got to our sixth home, it was a keeper: our dream antique home that we were able to purchase outright without a mortgage. When our monthly mortgage bills vanished, we put the same mortgage-payment cash flow into other wealth-building investments. It was a wonderful feeling.

▶ WHAT TAX BREAKS CAN I EXPECT WITH HOME OWNERSHIP?

Your home receives unique treatment under the tax code. The interest on your mortgage is a deduction that can be used against your income. In most states you may deduct real estate property taxes as well. Let's say you are in the 30 percent tax bracket and have a $250,000 mortgage at 5.5 percent. Each year you can deduct approximately $13,750 of interest from your income, which means a savings of $4,125 (0.03 x $13,750 = $4,125). Tax savings are really additional income.

There are also many government programs that come and go, such as first-time homebuyer's credit, solar equipment credits, energy-efficiency credits, and others too numerous to list. These benefits are creating wealth that you cannot access if you do not own a home. Ask your real-estate broker what tax breaks are available in the community where you are buying.

▶ SHOULD I BUY A SECOND HOME?

Second or vacation homes are a compilation of good and bad elements. Unlike a first or primary home, my rule of thumb is that you need a down payment of 50 percent of the purchase price to consider this expenditure. There are other factors involved. The worst part is that a second home is generally far from your primary residence and you cannot keep close tabs on it. Vandalism, weather damage, animal infestation, heating issues, or a host of other problems inevitably require your attention at inopportune times. You may also find that going to the same spot year after year loses its appeal, leaving the house empty most of the time. That said, the median price of a vacation home in 2007 was $195,000, so it is often not as expensive as your primary residence.

You cannot rent your vacation home as you can a true investment property. While you may be able to cover most of its out-of-pocket costs, that will ignore the *opportunity cost*. That is the value of what you had to give up in order to acquire equity in a second home. Opportunity cost is not a cash cost in a strict sense, but it should be part of your thinking when you do a cost-benefit analysis prior to buying a vacation home. If you had to make a down payment of $100,000, then you should at least consider what that amount might earn if it were invested elsewhere in your portfolio. If you are able to achieve 6.5 percent in a high-grade corporate bond, that is $6,500 of income per year that might compound over ten or more years. This is a significant sum.

So factor opportunity cost into the decision to buy a vacation home, along with the uniqueness of the property, its appeal to your family, the possibility of appreciation over a long period of time, and the diversification it may offer to your overall net worth. You are, after all, working hard to live the life you want. And at some level of wealth, the benefit of satisfaction becomes more important than the opportunity cost.

REAL ESTATE IS THE MIGRAINE EPICENTER OF INVESTING

"It's tangible, it's solid, it's beautiful. It's artistic, from my standpoint, and I just love real estate."

–DONALD TRUMP

If you wish to own investment real estate, you need a wonderful sense of humor to survive the travails of this kind of investing. Mr. Trump left out the fact that markets shift with cyclical bubbles, prices gyrate, real estate needs constant attention, buildings are in continual need of repair, and tenants are often mischievous and unreliable. Unlike you or me, Trump has an army of people to absorb the aggravation and do the hard work. If it were easy, the rewards would not be there. Everyone would do it profitably. In 2009, that myth was exploded by the number of smart people overextended in speculative real estate projects.

The most famous reference to real estate investing is that you should buy it because "they aren't making any more of it." To that the facts say, "hogwash!" If you buy a strip of tiny stores with limited parking because it's a great rural location and a developer builds a modern mall two miles down the road, you may end up with an unwanted island as traffic roars past you on the way to the mall. They *are* making more of "it," and the ways in which that can be done are endless. We cannot attempt to cover all the basics here, so this caution will be the main insight for you to take away.

Our focus is on a wealth-building **PLAN** that most people can adopt on a lifelong journey to their own level of financial security. The subject of real estate can fill many books and there is a wealth of information available on the Internet for study. In our **PLAN** we can only discuss the most common real estate that the normal family investor will encounter. So in addition to your family home, we will only briefly consider three kinds of real estate investing:

- Real estate investment trusts
- Sole rental ownership
- Real estate limited partnerships

If you get rich enough and want to own some large pieces of commercial property on your own, there are plenty of brokers and courses to help you gain expertise in this most complex of investing fields. My only caveat is that you stay away from creative financing sources and never do anything you don't thoroughly understand. Those who failed to heed this admonishment and bought "investment" condos and marginal strip malls during the credit bubble prior to the crash in 2008 most likely wish they had been more prudent. For many people, investing without expertise has wiped out their family fortune and will affect them for many years to come.

REAL ESTATE INVESTMENT TRUSTS

A *Real Estate Investment Trust* (REIT) is a special type of investment in real estate (and mortgages) that is like a mutual fund because of its property diversification. REITs have their own distinct attributes. They are often specialized in a particular type of property such as apartments, strip malls, industrial factories, hotels, parking lots, or office buildings. Unlike a mutual fund, a REIT is required to distribute 90 percent of its income, not including capital gains, in the form of dividends to shareholders. A REIT must invest at least 75 percent of its total assets in real estate and has to have 75 percent of its income stem from rents on the properties or mortgages. REITs make sense for individuals who are seeking to own investment properties but don't want the headache associated with individual ownership. They allow everyone who buys shares to reap some of the rewards of actually owning larger properties.

REITs hold three major advantages over sole ownership of a property:

- They offer liquidity. You can cash out at your option, selling your shares anytime you need the funds. As we mentioned earlier in our discussion of the *liquidity scale*, real estate itself is very illiquid, as you must find a buyer, negotiate a contract, and wait for a closing to free up your investment capital. It's a long process that can take months or, in the case of a bad market, years.
- REITs also offer management by experienced professionals who may be very familiar with a specific market.
- Finally, when you buy real estate through a REIT, you are not on the hook for a mortgage loan and the maximum you can lose is your investment.

REITs have several disadvantages:

- The biggest is that REITs do not pay income taxes, so any gain you receive is fully taxable income. The lower capital-gains tax rates that apply to stocks or bonds after they are held for a year never come into play—you will be taxed at your current income tax rate.
- Another problem with REITs is that they tend to specialize in a particular kind of property and thus can suffer significantly when that industry falls on hard times.
- Lastly, be sure to examine the leverage in a REIT (read this as debt level). If it is using so much debt that its leverage is higher than 60 percent, look for another one. On average, REITs have about 50 percent leverage. You don't want to own one that is borderline creditworthy.

If you decide that a REIT investment is for you, consider owning it within an IRA or other qualified tax plan to defer the tax bite. I do not like mortgage REITs for our safe and secure **PLAN** as they were dangerous to own in the financial meltdown of 2008. Besides, you can often do just as well from an income basis in bonds that have a very strong credit backing. If you want to own REITs, the limit should be approximately 3–5 percent of your portfolio.

REAL ESTATE LIMITED PARTNERSHIPS

Partnerships in real estate are investment vehicles in which two groups of people join together to purchase a larger property. The first group locates the property and writes an *offering memorandum* describing the transaction in detail. This first group is called the *general partner(s)*, which may consist of one or more people or corporations who generally sponsor the purchase, manage it, and seek funding for it. The general partners contact other investors and ask them to purchase parts of the investment in the original transaction. The personal liability for the outcome rests on the shoulders of the general partners, who are usually compensated with annual fees and a percentage ownership in the limited partnership.

The second group is the *limited partners* who are the investors, and their entire responsibility begins and ends with their investment. They are much like the shareholders of a corporation or REIT who have their money at risk but do not expose any other part of their portfolio of assets. Limited partners are not active in any phase of managing the property. All of this is spelled out in detail in the offering memorandum that gives the details of the property to be purchased, financial projections on expected profits, and the duties of each group.

Real-estate investment projects that focus on a specific property can sometimes be a very attractive investment. They have a high potential for growth, income distribution, and a variety of tax benefits. Generally speaking, a limited partnership is not for a beginning or intermediate investor, but is rather more suitable for a portfolio with excellent diversification and alternative cash flow. You will need some skill in evaluating the track record and reputation of the general partner, the *pro forma financials* (projections of what is expected but not guaranteed), and the type of property itself.

I have invested in several limited partnerships after rejecting hundreds, and reaped very handsome returns. The normal investment unit is $50,000 to $250,000, minimum. The many firms that make their living sponsoring such projects are easy to locate through a financial advisor or even the Internet. In any case, part of your due diligence should involve going out and physically inspecting the property prior to signing up. Never invest relying solely on a paper proposal.

Look for well-established general partners that have been in the business at least fifteen years and done numerous limited partnerships. The quality of the general partner is as important as the quality of the real estate. Examine the fee structure and how the general partner is compensated. The limited partners should have first call on income and profits before distributions to the general partner. Determine if the yearly management fee is reasonable.

The big drawback with a limited partnership is that the units you purchase are almost completely illiquid if you want out early. Since you are really locked in, plan on seeing this type of real-estate investment through to the final distribution.

SOLE RENTAL OWNERSHIP IS OFTEN SOUL OWNERSHIP

One morning when you have a bit of financial security, you awaken deciding to buy one or more rental properties. In theory, you as the landlord will be able to service the mortgage from its rental income, in time paying off the balance while benefiting from significant increasing equity and a continued stream of retirement income.

That is the textbook explanation of how rental units are supposed to perform. A couple of things are left out of this picture. Rental properties you acquire as a sole owner are work, aggravation, and risk at an advanced level that is as great, or greater, than almost any other investment except perhaps the stock market. That does not mean you have to avoid them completely in our **PLAN**. However, you should go into this investment opportunity with your eyes wide open.

We bought a run-down eight-family apartment in a town about

twenty miles from our home. Our goal was to fix up one apartment at a time and increase rents each time we placed the freshly remodeled unit back on the market. Over time the entire building would be modernized and its value would appreciate. That, at least, was the plan.

The first-floor apartment was the largest, so we began there: new kitchen cabinets and appliances, all-new bathroom, better windows, fresh paint. We rented the unit to what appeared to be a nice couple. The next step was to replace all of the hall doors, install smoke detectors, and plaster and repaint the hallways. We also decided to provide a laundry room in the basement and purchased a new coin-operated washer and dryer for our tenants' convenience.

One evening the fire department called us to the building. The wife of the nice couple on the first floor, being twice the size of her husband, had thrown him through one of the new windows. The damage was significant and there was blood all over the inside and outside walls. The fight had also damaged the newly renovated apartment. These tenants moved immediately and since they had no assets, we were left with a small security deposit that did not begin to cover the damage.

In another incident, a tenant returned home after a celebration in a local bar and used a claw hammer to redecorate the newly plastered and painted hallway. He also attempted to remove the doorknobs from all the new doors, leaving gouges in each door and jamb. All of that exertion must have left him thirsty because he proceeded to hammer off the coin boxes on the new washer and dryer for booze money. Once again, there was no point in trying to recover damages from a renter who vanished into the night. I might add that all of these tenants checked out fine when they applied for the lease (as far as a landlord is allowed to investigate tenant background under the law).

In another building we bought, we inherited a tenant with a

long lease. He failed to pay the rent for three months. After sending the appropriate notices to no avail, we finally went to visit. We found him dirty and unshaven, lying on the floor amidst his drug equipment. His eyeballs had almost vanished to where just the whites of his eyes showed. Food, dirty dishes, ashtrays full of cigarettes, and garbage were strewn everywhere. Although we notified the police, they couldn't do much to help. Our lawyer worked with us to evict the tenant but informed us we could not recount the actual scene in court as he could sue us because we had no tangible proof. All we could say was that the rent was overdue. He showed up with a lawyer, in a tie and jacket with a haircut and a shave. His version: he was laid off (we were told he was fired) and we, the rapacious landlords, were hounding him for money. The judge looked at us as though we had two heads and allowed him two more months of free rent before he had to move. Meanwhile, we had to pay our mortgage for those five months plus a substantial bill to clean up and refresh the apartment. As a parting gift, he left a lot of damage to the unit.

There are many great and responsible tenants out there. You will have them in most cases and your sole-ownership property will cruise along as planned. But you must be prepared for incidents like the ones I have just described and have the time, patience, and funds to deal with them. Anyone who has owned rental property has similar stories. There is money to be made in this type of investment, but it does not come without effort. However, if you purchase a property large enough that it is economic to pay a rental agent to service the rental units and their tenants, you can be somewhat insulated from the worst parts of a sole-ownership real-estate investment.

Sole-ownership property is part of our PLAN if you recognize it is hard work and risky. It can be a successful second job as long as the location is correct, your mortgage is reasonable, and you use appropriate professional lawyers, insurance agents, repair folks, and documents. Read a book on the subject of rental property. Make sure you can do minor repairs yourself, or the costs will hurt your cash flow. Speak to real-estate brokers, many of whom have had the experience. Recognize that landlords and tenants are on different sides of the table and sole-ownership real estate is a business and must be run like one.

You may wish to consider purchasing smaller starter houses to rent—the number of tenants will be fewer and turnover may be reduced. The only caveat there is don't go into partnership with a friend or family member. The extra problems associated with potential disagreements add a layer of complication it is best to avoid. As we stated in an earlier chapter, it's you baby … it's you!

7. WHERE SAFE AND SECURE WON'T GO

INVESTING NO-NOS

We will not go into any great detail on the following types of no-no investments, but instead list them with a brief description:

- *Hedge funds:* These are funds that are exempt from the strict rules and regulations that govern mutual funds, stocks, and bonds. They use very aggressive strategies including many elements that are not part of our **PLAN**, such as selling short, high leverage, program trading, swaps, arbitrage, and derivatives. In general the only hedge you should buy will have flowers in the spring and need trimming in the fall. Hedge funds, with their stiff fees (2 percent yearly of assets and 20 percent of the gains-, none of the losses), are not the way for most investors to make money. If you become very sophisticated, achieve a lot of assets, and do your homework, there may be a place for some hedge-fund investing as a small part of your portfolio. Just remember you are turning over complete control of your money to another person to invest.

- *Derivatives:* These are investments that gamble on the future price of assets such as currency, corn, hog bellies, and lots of other things you probably know nothing about.

- *Uncle Joe's start-up company:* I'm sure that you love Uncle Joe and he means well. But unless you are working in his business in a position of responsibility, take a pass. According to a *Money Magazine* survey, 43 percent of readers who lent money to family weren't paid back in full and 27 percent "hadn't received a dime." Sorry, Uncle Joe, but unless there is collateral and you agree on terms far more attractive than a safe corporate bond, you'll have to look elsewhere.

- *Captive mutual funds:* These are the mutual funds that are sold by certain institutions whose primary business is not in the promotion and successful management of mutual funds. A good example is the case history of Bank of America: its wealth-management services sold funds to investors and then did not look out for their welfare. On September 3, 2003, Eliot Spitzer (then New York's Attorney General) announced the issuance of a complaint against the hedge fund company Canary Capital Partners LLC, charging that they had engaged in "late trading" in collusion with Bank of America's Nations Funds. Bank of America was charged with permitting Canary to purchase mutual fund shares after the markets had closed, at the closing price for that day—a practice that harmed regular investors. Contrast that to

mutual fund giants like Fidelity Investments, American
Funds, Franklin Templeton, or Vanguard, whose primary
business is competitive mutual funds that are fee sensitive and well managed. (For some entertaining reading,
look up the history of Bank of America's loaded fees,
poor management, illegal trading, and terrible results
for investors. Bank of America is a bank. It's best in lending prowess but doesn't rank in the top twenty in mutual
fund assets.)

▪ *Timeshares*: This is a quasi-real estate joint ownership of
a vacation spot by many people who occupy it for short
periods during the calendar year. Timeshares often have
high yearly maintenance fees and are illiquid to sell once
you tire of going to the same place each year at the same
time. Rent a room or condo for your vacation and let
someone else tie up their money.

▪ *Commodity trading*: This is the purchase of the right to
buy tangible products like corn, copper, pork, beef, and
oil in the futures market. You have the right, but not
the obligation. You are betting on a price trend. These
markets are for professionals. In general, you don't know
enough about the commodity and what is happening
to gamble your hard-earned money. The one exception
might be precious metals such as gold or silver. I would
only buy a SPDR Gold Holding ETF (symbol: GLD) or
SPDR Silver Holding ETF (symbol: SLV) and not the underlying commodities themselves.

▪ *Annuities*: These contracts, sold by an insurance company, are designed to provide regular payments of a set
amount at set frequencies. The payments usually take
effect after retirement. The earnings on annuities are
allowed to accumulate tax free, but for the most part

investors receive a low yield. These instruments are loaded with fees for the insurance company (and their salespeople) and have lots of rules to lock in your years of investment. The surrender charges if you want out could choke a horse—no, make that a whole corral of horses. The last pleasant attribute is if you leave the annuity to your heirs, their tax bill may be so high they might have to sell other assets just to cover it.

■ *Whole life insurance:* This type of insurance combines a term policy (which pays a face amount to a beneficiary) with an investment component. The premiums you pay yearly are invested by the insurance company and may turn a profit that will belong to you. This profit may be counted as a decrease in the overall cost of the policy. But there may never be a profit, so you can't count on it as a sure thing. The investment component is supposed to build value (called *cash value*) by investing in stocks, bonds, or other instruments as specified in the policy. The theory is that you can borrow against this cash value if you need to do so. But you are paying not only for insurance, but for a series of fees and high commissions for the investment portion.

If the companies were good at investing, it might be worth the expense. However, they usually aren't. Agents will cite the forced savings aspect of regular premium payments, but in our **PLAN** regular savings are an important element of wealth creation—we don't need an insurance company forcing us to save. There are many better and cheaper ways to save for retirement. Stick with simple term insurance to cover your needs.

■ *Foreign real estate*: There are a host of reasons that make foreign real estate unattractive. The value of each nation's currency profoundly affects the value of its real estate in dollar terms. Foreign properties are difficult, expensive, and time consuming to physically get to with the whole family. Like a vacation home, you may decide you do not want to return to the same spot each and every year. As a foreign owner you may be subject to a byzantine series of regulations that don't allow you to repatriate profits to the United States even if the property appreciates in value. Lastly, if you die with foreign property in your estate, it can be a big headache for your heirs. The main advantage to foreign real estate is diversification out of the dollar, but the same goal can be accomplished with financial instruments.

- *Tax shelters*: In this case we are referring to any investment vehicle that purports to reduce taxable income more than $1 in tax for each $1 spent. Most tax shelters are at best questionable and at worst illegal. Their downfall usually stems from a valuation of some asset above or below its fair market value. When the purpose is to lower tax liability rather than to meet an economic opportunity, people end up going to jail. It's not worth playing in this pond.

- *Initial public offerings*: The debutante ball for a public company is the first day it is traded on a market, called the *initial public offering* (IPO). This very complex process governed by the Securities and Exchange Commission and investment bankers is designed to attract investors. Brokers are paid much larger commissions on most IPOs, so they push them very hard. A long and complex document called a *prospectus* contains a huge amount of information that very few can decipher and fewer still use to make a rational decision. Although

the offering price for shares in the newly public company can rise very quickly, it often ends up dropping like
a stone. I don't ever buy on the first day or even the first
month. It's best to avoid this investment until you see
how things shake out.

8

INSURANCE

PLANNING ON HEALTH TO KEEP WEALTH

Insurance is a cost of doing business—the business of living, raising a family, and helping to secure future generations. When a close friend of our family was thirty-six years old with a five-year-old son, her liver suddenly failed due to a hepatitis infection, and she needed an expensive transplant. Her family had wisely carried a top-of-the-line health plan that picked up large medical costs with a very high total limit. Good thing. Her transplant procedure turned out not to be routine, and she spent twenty-two days in intensive care with round-the-clock nursing coverage. The hospital, surgical, and organ-tissue-acquisition bills arrived in a box and totaled a staggering $934,000. Yes, you read that correctly. It cost a million dollars, and if her health coverage had not been sufficient, our friend and her family would be paying off the medical debt for the rest of their lives.

Even if you believe you are invincible, you need high-quality health insurance as part of a basic financial plan. Consider it diversification of risk and get adequate coverage for yourself and your family. Most people are covered by an employer-based plan, but if you lose your job there is the danger that you will not qualify for an individual policy. Once you are unemployed, your ship may be sunk. Acquiring individual insurance is nothing short of a nightmare if you have less-than-perfect health or if the large premiums are difficult or impossible to pay with no salary coming in. However, the risk of no or skimpy coverage can lead to ruinous medical expenses from which it may be impossible to recover. Insurance premiums need to be part of your rainy-day fund planning even with the new health care law.

Everyone needs to be careful when purchasing health plans because both small companies and brand-name giants sell a wide range of coverage. Many plans have gaping holes and weak coverage in catastrophic situations. Here are some tips to consider:

1. Know in advance what your out-of-pocket responsibility might be in a major medical situation. A good policy will have a cap on what you pay and then begin covering 100 percent of the costs.

2. Review a history of premium increases from the company over the last decade.

3. Never buy a product that is labeled as a "limited" benefit—that is a sure sign that there are holes in the plan.

4. Lower premiums mean lower benefits. Period. The only way to trim what you pay is to trim what you get.

5. If the plan begins medical coverage on the second day of an illness or hospitalization, look elsewhere. Most of the expense is likely to come on the first day in an acute situation.

6. Understand how diagnostics are covered.

7. If you have a ceiling on the per-day payment, know what you are getting into. A maximum of $1,200 per day may seem like a lot until you consider our friend's bill. She spent more than $42,000 per day on average once her eleven-hour surgery and subsequent eight-hour surgery were factored in.

8. Deal with a reputable agent who has been in business a long time. We all know that Woody Allen quote, "There are worse things in life than death. Have you ever spent an evening with an insurance salesman?" Still, you do need a good agent, so look for a Charter Life Underwriter.

9. Good coverage should cover the entire process until you are fully recovered. This includes the front end at the hospital as well as prescriptions, outpatient follow-up, radiation treatment, rehabilitation, and medical equipment such as wheelchairs or crutches.

There are excellent resources online to calculate how much you are likely to spend for the coverage you need. One of the best is http://www.ehealthinsurance.com/, which evaluates your zip code, age, gender, individual and family plans, and some other variables in an easy online program. You will be able to compare quotes safely and securely without an agent being present. It also helps you to understand the government program, which is set to come into existence in 2014. However, it would still be a wise idea to compare your considered plan against one that an agent or the government attempts to sell. Do the research and then get it in writing.

Don't become aware of your limits on medical coverage once it is too late. If you only look at price, expect the possibility you might have to pay handsomely at some point in the future. Read the fine print. All of it. The insurance companies profit from the confusion around health insurance and state regulators do a poor job of protecting you. No one really knows the final form of the government health care program set to be introduced in 2014 so assume for now it may not benefit you.

With the lack of standard definitions for commercial contracts, the devil is in the details. You should have the medical care you need at the moment that you need it. The only way to get it is with advanced preparation. Otherwise all the rest of your financial planning can be for naught.

Insuring your property and life is another cornerstone of our overall **PLAN** of safe and secure.

1. Property insurance

Property insurance is rather straightforward. It may include policies on homes, investment properties, autos, art, antiques, and the like. There are many perils in the world and it pays to join a pool of people with a profile like your own, who are individually unlikely to have a loss but collectively participating to fund a member's loss should it occur.

Hundreds of companies offer many forms of property insurance, including:

- **Real estate**: Our **PLAN** favors a replacement policy because it guarantees that the insurer will replace a loss with the same kind of building. So if you have a fire in your home and lose it together with its contents, you won't spend years arguing with the insurer about depreciation and value on what you owned before the loss.
- **Jewelry, art, and antiques**: The insurer can only give money and not replace the objects lost. I suggest getting an appraisal every five or so years to keep pace with changes in value due to inflation or market forces.
- **Auto insurance**: Carry very high coverage limits that protect you and your assets from lawsuits in case a severe automobile accident is your fault.

In each of these cases, a higher *deductible*, which is the portion you pay of a claim, will help to keep down premium payments. The more of a claim you are willing to pay, the less exposure an insurer has. That reduced risk means charging you less. So if you are comfortable with a $1,000, $5,000, or $10,000 deductible expect the policy cost to reflect what you cover by charging less for additional responsibility placed on the insured. That's easy.

2. Life insurance

Life insurance is what you buy until your assets are extensive enough to guarantee the financial future regardless of subsequent events. At that point of financial security, you will find that some of the yearly premium may be better invested elsewhere. Then as your estate continues to grow, you may buy insurance again to help pass on the assets you worked so hard to acquire and want your descendants to enjoy.

Life insurance is where you need a real professional to run projections that reflect your life and circumstances. When you are young and single, you probably don't need life insurance. However, the need for coverage tracks pretty much with the responsibilities you add during your life. The starting point is usually when you get married and have a child. Then you have to plan as best you can to fund your family's future in the event of your premature and unpredictable demise. Choose a reputable company that will be around to honor the insurance contract. The trick is not to buy way more coverage than necessary. Don't forget our future value calculations when you are trying to ascertain the amount of financial need.

Life insurance comes in two flavors:

■ *Term life insurance* is purchased for a specific number
of years and then ends. It can sometimes be renewed at
a different premium level (you are older) and perhaps

for a shorter number of years (you are more likely to become ill the older you get). Term insurance is substantially cheaper and you are hoping to lose the bet that you die prematurely, but will leave your family more secure if you do kick the bucket.

- *Whole life insurance lasts as long as you contin*ue to pay all the required premiums and builds a fantasy asset called *cash value.* The policy itself has an internal investment account that builds up this cash value over the years. I call it a fantasy because the whole purpose of a lifetime life insurance policy is to keep it until you die. When you do, the cash value is gone and the policy pays out the contract face amount. You can borrow against cash value while the insurance is in force, but the loan is unlikely to be your cheapest and best source of funds.

Whole life policies are significantly more expensive than term life policies. The insurance company is collecting lots of fees on your "savings" portion. If the purpose of insurance is to protect against a specific event, then it seems logical to use the additional premium dollar cost of whole life over term insurance to either buy more term life insurance or invest the funds yourself elsewhere. There are many different kinds of cash value insurance products including universal life, variable universal life, variable whole life, single-premium life, and second-to-die life. Have your insurance agent explain them. Then forget about whole life insurance and choose the cheapest term life insurance from a highly rated carrier. You can find out the ratings of insurers at www.ambest.com/ratings or www.lifeinsurancestar.com. As for my opinion of whole life, I believe it is just a poor way to go and term life will almost always serve you better.

3. Disability insurance

Disability insurance replaces lost income if a wage earner can no longer work. We will not spend a lot of time discussing all the angles of this sometimes expensive coverage. Physical disability derails our **PLAN** for wealth acquisition and forces a rethink of your life's possibilities. Some financial planners think this type of insurance is very important, but I feel a catastrophic event that leaves you disabled must inevitably lead to the use of other safety nets such as Social Security and family members. Very few workers can purchase enough disability insurance to replace all current income lost, so major life adjustments will probably have to be made to modify living standards in any case.

Even though most people are three times more likely to be disabled than to die prematurely, I am on the fence about disability insurance. I think that a little is OK, but you don't need to cover every cent of income. The judgment call is up to you. Some coverage at vulnerable phases of your life (such as with small children) may be wise, but when a family has created wealth with income, disability insurance is not really necessary.

If you do opt for some kind of disability coverage, avoid any plan that pays only if you can't work at all. Those policies are sometimes interpreted so if you can qualify as the local dog catcher the insurer will argue you are not completely disabled. The policy should be directed at your own occupation and not just a catchall, which pays no benefit if you can still drive the community dog wagon (or wash dishes).

Also keep in mind that statistically women live longer than men, so expect female disability coverage to be somewhat more expensive. The place to start your investigation of disability coverage is with your employer, who might have some sort of policy as a benefit package. You can purchase your own additional coverage if you wish, but deal only with top-rated companies. The Web site www.lifehappens.org has a full explanation of this product and a disability "insurance needs calculator" to help you explore the various options.

4. Umbrella Insurance

Umbrella policies are a cheap method to secure your assets in today's litigious environment without significant cost. They begin to protect you after you have exhausted other liability coverage under your car and homeowners insurance. So their deductible is usually $250,000 or more and that makes them very inexpensive. Almost everyone should have an umbrella policy because the cost is so low (around $250 for the first $1 million) and the protection of your assets is basic to our safe and secure PLAN. In the very rare event you are sued and forced to pay a legal settlement, the umbrella policy will save your hard-earned assets and not subject you to a lifetime of payments from your income.

9

ENTREPRENEURSHIP—
DREAM IT, DO IT

Entrepreneurship is a calling. If you have reached this point in our book and understand most of our investing **PLAN**, it is reasonably certain that you have the stuff to become an entrepreneur. I always knew that was where my career would take me because early on I came to trust my own judgment. Don't misunderstand and think that I believed my solution was always the right answer. Instead, I felt that no matter what state of affairs happened to come along, it was possible to calmly analyze athe problem and pose a possible fix. Sometime things worked and other times the action was not correct. Still, I learned much more from failure than could be learned from success.

It does not matter if the economy is bleak, the administration in Washington is unfriendly to business, how convoluted the regulations are, or if all of your friends think that the safe way (a salaried job) is the best route to earning a living. What matters is your research, your idea, and a positive conviction in your analytical skill. The rest is plain old hard work.

One of the interesting methods I have employed to gain knowledge or facts on a project is to dress down (no designer suit or expensive tie) and ask experts for advice. You can sometimes pose as a student (MBA, law) doing a research paper and approach the most successful of people to briefly review a one-page summary you have written or discuss a particular point. My experience is that people *want* to be helpful and give input. The key is that it needs to be done in person because wealthy people have screeners (secretaries, assistants, etc.) to guard their time. You have to get through that layer for a face-to-face. (I know of a graduate with an Ivy League MBA who hired an actor and sent him to the office of an executive with his resume on a silver platter. That got him an interview where normal human resources channels never even got him a rejection letter. That's entrepreneurship in job location.)

The real truth is that the best way to create wealth is to follow a good business plan doing something you love. But do keep in mind Jim Allchin's excellent example. He spent sixteen years at Microsoft being responsible for many platform components until he retired in 2007 and became a professional musician who released his first album in 2009. Go after what you want. Starting and building a business is a huge financial gamble that can take years to accomplish. Setbacks are inevitable and working hours long. But if your heart is in it, then you have a shot.

If you have been sitting in a cubicle for much of your career believing that your forty-hour workweek is tough, the shock of a one hundred-hour workweek will be a wakeup call if you break out on your own. And if you do hit the ball out of the park but then want to captain a fishing boat … well, like Jim Allchin, you can.

Only you can judge if the moment and your idea are right. Here are some questions to aid in your evaluation:

1. Are your spouse and family behind you 100 percent?
2. Can you give up your present lifestyle for years while you build the company?
3. Are you aware of your shortcomings as well as skills in management?

4. Is your judgment good enough to trust decisions that you have to make quickly?
5. Do you have a persuasive personality to win others over?
6. Will your educational background give you an edge?
7. Is confidence a part of your nature so that a loss won't shatter your self-esteem?
8. Have you done your homework and rechecked it again and again?
9. Do you want a partner or do you work best alone?
10. Do you have the contacts required to execute the business plan?
11. Is your energy level high?

For safety's sake remember to keep the **rainy-day fund** reserve untouched. That way, if things do not work out as planned, you still have some resources to support your family while you re-enter the more conventional business world. The rainy-day part of your **PLAN** never goes away if you are to be safe and secure. Bankruptcy is never a pleasant option for you and those you are responsible for.

There are many Web sites that can give you valuable free information on start-up businesses. Use the Internet in your due diligence process. Some interesting sites are:

1. *www.entrepreuneur.gov:* This blog is supported by the Kauffman Foundation. It focuses on issues of innovation and has an extensive repository of articles, videos, and other media. There is online education with input from some of the most successful entrepreneurs.
2. *www.entrepreneurmagazine.com:* While this site has some useful tips, it doesn't contain a lot of hard content. Nevertheless, it provides a useful overview, and the ads tell you a lot about the marketplace.

3. *www.franchise.com:* Explore franchising as an option to get a good overview of what others have done. If you need the support a high-quality franchise organization can give, go to this site for its good directory and some insight as to what is going on in the market. But keep in mind they are trying to sell you something.

4. *www.sba.gov/smallbusinessplanner/plan/writebusinessplan/ index.html:* The Small Business Administration (SBA) provides an excellent road map to developing a comprehensive business plan. It goes step-by-step and has online workshops. The site has links to all the SBA programs.

5. *www.youtube.com/watch?v=hbysbP7Q0aM:* This eight-part video on business plans has some pointers. It's worth an hour to sit through.

6. *www.vfinance.com:* This site has a useful, and free, venture-capital-firm resource directory. So does www.capitalvector.com, but there is a fee to access listings.

You don't have to be the PhD inventor of the next generation of computer chips or the ultimate authority on a specific new product to succeed. Lots of millionaires made their fortunes selling hamburgers, coffee, cleaning agents, and silverware. Of course you must have a good concept of what a specific marketplace is ready to accept and pay for. Be aware that marketing is as much a component of success as what you sell. Don't underestimate the capital resources you will need to get your message to the buyers. Your business plan can be all about marketing if you find a franchise that has a quality product or service that meets a need in a particular market.

The Internet and television are powerful persuaders—you can launch a business more easily now than at any time in history because of great access to the public. How powerful are these two marketing vehicles? As Erma Bombeck says, "My children refuse to eat anything that has not danced on television."

I want to be encouraging. If you do start a successful business, the rewards are more than monetary. There is the great feeling of having taken a risk and made it pay off for you and your family. If you have the will, work hard, and use marketing channels successfully, there is a good chance you can attract the sales and build a new company.

10

LIVING (AND DYING)
WITH SUCCESS

WHAT YOUR FAMILY CAN TRUST

For many people the hard work of a lifetime can make a huge difference in the lifestyle of their progeny. Our country was built on the notion that it is possible to help children achieve more than was available to their parents and grandparents. Poorly educated immigrants who come to the United States often work hard to make the money that enables their children to attend university and perhaps become professionals. In the same vein, multigenerational progress is part of our **PLAN**, and trusts are a method of securing this effort.

At its most basic level, a *trust* is a legal arrangement that transfers control and responsibility for property to another person or institution. The trust is formed with the help of a lawyer by an individual who gives *fiduciary control* away so that the property transferred will be used for the benefit of the *beneficiaries*, the persons stipulated in the *trust agreement*. A fiduciary, often called a *trustee*, has a legal and ethical responsibility to carry out the wishes of the *grantor*, the person establishing the trust. It is possible to have someone you know and have confidence in as the trustee, but it is just as common to appoint a corporate trust company or a bank to serve in that role. The advantage in having an institution in this role is that it does not age like an individual and may have a much higher understanding of trust administration. But institutions charge substantial fees and are sometimes mired in red tape and bureaucratic processes.

No matter what some people may think, the most successful device for independence is money. That is how we should approach the topic of why you need to become familiar with trusts. Trusts you have, or trusts you establish for others, offer choice and a certain amount of financial bedrock. Our **PLAN** pushes young people toward leaving the world a little better than they found it. Correctly established, a trust provides ammunition for social achievements along the lines of great business leaders such as Gates, Rockefeller, Morgan, and a host of others. Their foresight in the use of their money helped both their descendants and the rest of society.

As we present it, trusts aren't set up to rob initiative and promote indolence. It's the combination of industriousness and money that transforms good intentions into tangible reality for people and worthy institutions. A trust can be a helpful push to achieve your goals and also offer a shell of protection.

If you decide that setting up a trust is the way to go, discuss it with legal counsel. The establishment and use of trusts is a complex area of wealth creation and management. Here's an overview of six kinds of trusts:

1. LIVING TRUSTS

The *living trust* is established during the grantor's lifetime. It can be *revocable* (changed or cancelled) or *irrevocable* (cannot be changed in any way once it is established). A living trust is often created in the context of estate planning to allow assets to be sheltered from estate taxes or to maintain privacy. When you become a high net-worth individual, these goals may be very important. However, living trusts are also useful for managing assets while you are alive and distributing them properly after your death. Your estate is your family's treasure chest. Passing on its contents in an efficient manner is a complex process that should be coordinated by a legal advisor who follows the latest twists and turns in the law.

2. TESTAMENTARY TRUSTS

The *testamentary trust* arises from the grantor's will at the point of death. In this case the *testator* (also called the *settler*) specifies in a will document what will happen to all or part of the estate accumulated during a lifetime. The trustee will oversee the trust until it expires. Testamentary trusts are often created to protect a surviving spouse or minor children until they reach a certain age or accomplish an event such as college graduation or marriage. The testator can't be there, but is attempting to meet the needs of another person. It is common for the testator to write a *letter of direction* for the trustee, although in most cases the trustee has discretion to apply assets as the will specifies and in any lawful manner. The testamentary trust may easily be changed by altering the will and is not generally a tool for managing estate taxes.

3. CHARITABLE REMAINDER TRUST

A *charitable remainder trust* is an irrevocable entity the trustee sets up to provide income for a beneficiary for a specified period. Once the trust terminates, the remainder is given to a charity or other entity. The charitable remainder trust can be set up during your lifetime or can source from a provision in your will. If you become wealthy enough to fund a family foundation, this may be your tool. It is also an excellent way to repay a university or other charitable entity that provided help or comfort when you needed it.

4. IRREVOCABLE LIFE INSURANCE TRUST

A *life insurance trust* is created upon the death of the insured person so that a trustee will have assets from an insurance policy to invest and administer for the benefit of one or more beneficiaries. There are many interesting estate-tax benefits in this type of trust, which is usually established and coordinated with the purchase of the insurance policies. For the purposes of our **PLAN** for safe and secure investing, wealth creation with life insurance trusts can assure the availability of sufficient assets after an untimely death.

5. DYNASTY TRUST

A *dynasty trust* is a rather specialized trust that holds assets for the benefit of beneficiaries without transferring direct ownership of the assets to any beneficiary. It is used by donors who want to provide for many succeeding generations beyond their own children. Properly structured, a dynasty trust keeps assets so they can pass tax-free from one generation to another as long as your lineage continues. There is also no asset exposure to a beneficiary's creditors.

Appreciation of assets is generally exempt from estate and transfer taxes once all current rules have been complied with. In some states there are no state taxes to pay when the trust is set up. You don't need to be a resident of the more liberal states to set up your trust there, but this is a matter for tax counsel to deal with.

6. CHARITABLE LEAD TRUST

The *charitable lead trust* applies an income for a set period of time to a favorite charity and then returns the asset to the family treasure chest. It is a useful vehicle for accomplishing a specific goal.

In almost all cases trusts give some tax advantages to the donor, but keep in mind there is still a cost in giving away assets. Benefits may include savings in capital gains or estate taxes. The rather high level of estate taxation in the United States (37–55 percent) makes trust planning very attractive. Many people feel that if a stiff tax is paid at the time the assets were acquired, the mere passage of time until death should not give rise to a second large tax liability. Congress has not seen fit to see it that way. Trusts are a commonly used and well-defined vehicle to preserve your hard-earned money for many different purposes.

Trusts allow you to specifically direct how your assets should be used in ways that cannot be accomplished in a will. You can touch the future forever in a positive way. Proper planning can minimize fees and keep the miracle of compounding going on for what you cherish long after you have lost your earthly toehold. Isn't that what a successful and thoughtful individual would want? With luck, someone in your family has set up a trust that gives you a little boost. Explore the trust pathways to extend this helping hand to others.

WHAT DOES IT ALL MEAN

Our money **plan** likely will pay off over time for those willing to make the effort to implement it for themselves and their family. There are things that can disrupt its progress, such as divorce, illness, loss of major portions of assets, or a variety of other events. But when you stick with our three-legged stool over a long period of time, you have a very real chance of creating the wealth you desire. If you step back from the nitty-gritty of the execution methodology, I believe you will see that its most basic themes are just plain old common sense. They are a powerful combination of elements that I have tested over a lifetime.

11

THEMONEYPLANBOOK.COM

There is a very useful Web site that can be used by readers in conjunction with this book at **www.themoneyplanbook.com** for a number of purposes. Most of the forms for budgeting, Internet site references, and some additional information can be found there.

In addition, readers can post comments on material that is in the book or might be added to subsequent editions of the book. The author will check **www.themoneyplanbook.com** for those comments and may respond to specific posts.

INDEX